Living the Dream

THE FOUR PILLARS TO LIFE MASTERY

TRACY,
Always live your
Dreams + Grant
wishes to others!

Living the Dream

THE FOUR PILLARS TO LIFE MASTERY

PETER WALLIN

PETER WALLIN
607-857-6197
www.Pwallin.com

Printed in the United States of America

ISBN: 978-1-59571-515-9
Library of Congress Control Number: 2010922839

Designed and published by:
Word Association Publishers
205 Fifth Avenue
Tarentum, Pennsylvania 15084
www.wordassociation.com
1 800 827 7903

What the industry says about Peter Wallin and his "In Pursuit" series

FROM AMAZON.COM:

"This little book packs a big wallop! In nearly 30 years of reading business and self-help books, Peter's book is simply one of the best I've read. It's the most specific in delivering practical, pragmatic actions you can take now to fulfill your dreams. And it's written in clear straightforward, easy-to-understand language. Let this book be your first (or next) mentor. It's worth every bit of effort you'll put into implementing Mr. Wallin's recommendations. And they are SO worth implementing. As I'm taking my own life and career to another level, I'm using it as a refresher and guide. And having a lot of fun doing so!"

LORNA MCCLEOD, BOOK COACH, READING, CALIFORNIA

"5 Stars - Highly recommended as a supplementary guide for business owners and anyone pursuing a business career, especially in networking-dependent fields.

MIDWEST BOOK REVIEW, OREGON, WISCONSIN

“ • Pete is successful. Choose your definition of the word. He fills it.

• He became successful practicing what he writes about in his books.

• He writes with transparency. He is not phony or plastic.

• He is humble, continually giving credit to those from whom he learned.

• His books are written in plain English - no technical jargon. Glossary not necessary.

• No fluffy “new-paradigm” concepts to wade through. He shares practical, time-tested techniques for you to grow.

• What he shares in this book you can do. Yes, YOU.”

JEFF RYAN, RYAN AGENCY, HORNELL, NEW YORK

"There is only one way to master your life—to be able to live your life in your own way…"

PETER WALLIN

DEDICATION

For Michael, Peter, and Angela.
My love for you is immeasurable.

Acknowledgments

This book took a while to write. While my first book, *In Pursuit of Business*, was a collection of success stories from business people I interviewed, this second book is much more personal. It has taken me a lifetime to put it together. The whole concept of "Living, Giving, Sharing and Caring" isn't something that happens naturally. It takes effort. It takes hard work, nurturing of relationships and a lot of faith. I first began to see shades of it by watching my parents, Chuck and Lorraine Wallin. They've been married over 55 years! That doesn't happen without proper life balance of work, raising a family, and spending time together alone, appreciating everything in life.

Marilyn and I have been married almost a quarter of a century. While I worked and brought home the paycheck through the years, she stayed home with the kids and kept our house in order. In many ways I think she's grown more than I have. Our children, Michael, Peter, Jr., and Angela have learned the proper values in life, not just from listening to us but also from watching our daily actions. We are very transparent with our lives in everything we do—and it shows. For me to write this book, it's simply been a chance to recount the events in our lives that have formed us into the family we are today. (and since it's my book, I share the stories the way I remember them.)

I could not have completed this book without the support and encouragement of my friend Donna Kozik (mybigbusinesscard.com). You've been with me since the very beginning, and I've learned a great deal about writing and marketing from you. You are a very gifted writer yourself and you have made my work so much better. I also want to thank Kathy Felong for her timely advice and counsel. And to my publisher Tom Costello and designer Gina Datres, from Word Association Press, thanks for making this product look and feel professional. I'm looking forward to doing this all again sometime soon.

Finally, I'd like to thank my staff at Wallin Insurance Agency, Inc. Marlene Gerow, Linda Gessi, Jonna Holden, Shelly Cadek, Rose Forsyth and Lloyd Coble. You've certainly taken care of me through the years. I appreciate all you've done for my family and me.

Table of Contents

Introduction

Do you know people who are so involved with work that they aren't paying attention to what's going on at home? Do you see them get up on a Monday morning and turn on their "automatic pilot" button and begin yet another uneventful and unemotional week at their "ho-hum" job? When you see them again on a Friday afternoon, they're excited about the upcoming weekend, but they look tired, old, and even out of shape. They try to cram an entire week's worth of activities into a few short days, and it simply can't be done. They get frustrated and even depressed when they see Monday morning approaching again.

THE SUNDAY NIGHT BLUES

This is no way to live. It can lead to poor health, poor relationships, and a rapid decline in your personal well-being.

I have learned to live each and every day as if it is **the greatest day on earth.** I live one day at a time and focus on the things that are truly important to me: family, friendship, and the opportunity to meet new people, and help them with their problems. I know that my days are my own and I have learned to assume complete control over the actions I take and the responses I make.

Being **here in the moment** I know how important it is to learn from my past and then plan my upcoming day. Sure, I'm always looking to the future eagerly—for the goals I set for my life are compelling. I know my future is not guaranteed, but I also know only I can control my own thoughts about how I will handle whatever comes my way this day.

The reason I am writing this book is to share with you my own methods for success. I have broken it down into four pillars of emotional success – I call it Life Mastery - that I will share with you in these upcoming pages. Living positively and adhering to these pillars has become my definition of the **American Dream.**

I have more than two decades of experience working directly with both individuals and small businesses. I have amassed thousands of hours of experience in the fields of motivation, inspiration, and developing a deep sense of faith. I have built my own business up from the roots and have been lucky to enjoy peace and emotional tranquility along the way. I've learned to value the journey as much as the destination. And I've learned how to properly balance my work, my family, my social life, and my spiritual life.

It's a great feeling, and I can't wait to share it with you.

I've often been asked, "How can I be successful? What specifically should I do?" I think some people are looking for someone else to wave a magic wand and create a world of instant gratification and happiness.

My response in such situations is usually not the answer that's expected. That's because I believe it's the wrong question to start with. It's not important to know HOW to do something until you realize WHY you want to do it. By answering the "WHY," you will begin to understand the reasons for wanting certain things in your life.

I will help you discover WHY it's important to achieve certain things in your life—why you should do the things that will ultimately make a huge difference in your life, your work, and your commitment to others.

In this book I will reveal to you the four pillars of Life Mastery. In order, they are **Living, Giving, Sharing, and Caring.** Discover the importance of each and the critical nature that can bring you to levels of inner satisfaction far beyond your imagination.

Read on and find out how you can start your own journey toward deep personal satisfaction and a proper life-work balance.

To get the most out of this book, there is just one thing I ask of you, something more important than any technique or rule. If you abide by this you'll be well on your way to mastering your life and fulfilling your own dreams. And it is this:

You must have a deep, driving desire to improve your current situation—and an open mind to follow through.

You may discover that you already practice some of the principles of these four pillars discussed here. That's great! But ask yourself, Am I currently practicing them regularly? Make a commitment to put them into action. I will give you everything I have. So read on and apply these principles and practice them for yourself. I promise you'll like what you see.

ABOUT AUTHOR PETER WALLIN:

- Over two decades experience in the insurance industry—as a sales agent, sales manager, and successful owner of an independent operation
- Owner and president of Wallin Insurance Agency, Inc. Has earned numerous awards for profitability and sales
- Motivational speaker on topics like public speaking, customer service, and marketing
- Author of the book *In Pursuit of Business,* as well as the *In Pursuit of* ... series of audio products
- Community leader. Serves as Chairman of the Board for the United Way of the Southern Tier in New York, and has held leadership positions with the Chemung Sunrise Rotary, Meals on Wheels, Chemung County Chamber of Commerce, and the President's Council of Elmira College.
- Business leader. Serves as Chairperson of the Erie Insurance Marketing Task Force and is a founding member of The BEST Networking Group.
- Resides in Horseheads, New York, with wife, Marilyn, and their three children: Michael, Peter, Jr., and Angela.

PILLAR 1
In Pursuit of Living

"Do not follow where the path may lead; Go instead where there is no path and leave a trail."

RALPH WALDO EMERSON
(1803-1882) AMERICAN PHILOSOPHER AND POET

Chapter 1

LIFE BALANCE

"Buy a stock. If it goes up, sell it.
If it goes down, don't buy it."

YOGI BERRA
HALL OF FAME BASEBALL PLAYER AND MANAGER

Do you sometimes feel overwhelmed at work? So busy you can't take a break? Do you find yourself hanging out with co-workers and complaining about your job, your industry, and how tired you are when you get home at night? Do you often say, "I should have done that?" or "Why can't I seem to get a break?"

When you get home after another workday are you so wrapped up thinking about your job that you can't seem to relax? Do others around you sense that you are so preoccupied that you are not really "here" in the conversation?

I know the feeling; I've been there too. When I was working in the corporate world I often came home from a hard day only to have to "deal" with my wife Marilyn and our three kids (all under the age of 7). They would begin to tell me about their day, but I only half-listened. I was so exhausted from my own stressful day that I had little left in the tank for them.

Shortly after our third child, Angela, was born, I remember waking up to her crying in the middle of the night. I got up to give her a warm bottle of milk. I was feeling pretty proud of myself for "being a good dad." I was performing my duty! Marilyn got up to check on things.

I told her, "I never remember the boys crying in the middle of the night. They must have slept all the way through."

"Oh, no," Marilyn replied. "They were up crying every night for their bottle, but YOU never heard a thing. I fed them myself most of the time." She wasn't angry, just pointing out the fact that I was too self-absorbed.

It set off a warning bell, but not one I was ready to listen to quite yet. My priorities were mixed up. It was clear I had been more interested in my own agenda (sleep!) while Marilyn tended to the parenting duties at hand.

Another warning bell went off soon after. I was at one of my son Mikey's soccer games, back when he was very young. I was on my cell phone with a client. I was so involved in the call that I missed Mikey score a goal. There I was, standing on the sideline, but not really present. (Today, I can't even remember who I was talking to.) As a result, I missed the big goal. I saw the happy expression on Mikey's face afterward as the other parents congratulated me, but I missed the moment that mattered.

TIME TO CHANGE MY CAREER

When I was a sales manager for a large corporation I was making well into six figures. I was living a life of luxury—new cars, a motor home, and tickets to the Super Bowl—but the job itself was stressful. I had high sales quotas to reach and was expected to work 70 hours a week. Nights and weekends were often devoted to work. I was so exhausted I didn't have time to give my kids a hug before they went to bed.

I remember the company was demanding me to do more and more. More pressure to sell, recruit new salespeople, and hit sales targets no matter what it took. My home life suffered because I was rarely around, my health began to deteriorate, I gained weight, and I had very infrequent contact with friends outside of my industry. Marilyn and I rarely went out on a date, much less talk about the daily activities with the kids. I was losing sleep and I know I even started looking old, even though I was only in my mid-30s (yes, I was generating gray hair very quickly). I was struggling with the fact that I might have to live the rest of my life this way—or was I capable of creating a drastic change in my life and go out and try something completely new?

Then, one Saturday in June 1997, I was golfing with two of my best friends, Larry Piper and Jeff Ryan. The conversation came up about altering our careers and perhaps each of us beginning our own business as independent insurance agents. Erie Insurance was a relatively new company entering New York State, and they were looking to expand and appoint agents in our area. I casually began researching the possibility of opening my own business right here in Elmira, New York, representing Erie Insurance. Interestingly, Larry and Jeff had been experiencing similar problems dealing with a captive corporate mentality and their "company-comes-first" direction.

I spent six months exploring this opportunity. I began to look at the core of my problem: The balance in my life was off, but I now had a chance to do something about it. Yes, it meant quitting my high-paying job and starting something brand new (a "scratch" business). As I thought about it and prayed about it, something felt right. I felt a sense of peace and tranquility—I had a chance to take control of my situation and determine my own outcome.

I sat down with Marilyn and together we created a list of the priorities. We looked at creating a balance in our lives that honored family, good health, an accepting career, and giving back to our community. It wouldn't be easy and success wouldn't be immediate. We knew had to commit 100%, at all times, to keeping the priorities in balance by giving them time and proper attention.

"It's time to live the life you imagined"

HENRY JAMES, AUTHOR

We began to see impressive results in our attitudes—both on the inside and outside. We knew it wouldn't be easy, but with proper planning and working toward an improved life balance we felt good about ourselves. Somehow, the stress had already been lifted.

Over the years I have measured and monitored the categories in my life that I believe are critical to having a proper balance in my career, my home and my family. I've broken them down into the following five areas:

1. Current physical fitness
2. Work life
3. Intellectual and cultural interest
4. Community involvement
5. Career acceptance

I will share with you the things I have learned about myself and the improvements that I've made along the way. I can honestly tell you I now live an awesome life filled with rewards in all of these areas. I'm no longer missing my life, I'm living it.

LIVING THE DREAM

"It is the very pursuit of happiness that thwarts happiness."

VIKTOR FRANKL
(1905-1997) HOLOCAUST SURVIVOR AND AUTHOR OF *MAN'S SEARCH FOR MEANING*

CREATING A LIFE BALANCE

Knowing how I improved my own life has given me the strength to now be able to share with you. It begins with a very simple quiz, titled **"LIFE PLANNING FOR A BALANCED YOU."** I developed it several years ago after discovering the importance of gauging the priorities in my life.

I urge you to take the time and complete it—right now. Be honest; you're only cheating yourself if you're not. Once you're done we'll begin to look at things you can do immediately, right here and right now, to make dramatic improvements in your life.

Life Planning for a Balanced You

SCORE 1 POINT FOR EVERY **YES** ANSWER BELOW: (QUESTIONS 1-5)

PHYSICAL FITNESS **Y / N**

1. Do you participate in at least one organized sport (softball, bowling, tennis, etc.)? ___

2. Are you proficient? Do you consider yourself a good athlete and contributor to your team? ___

3. Do you participate in aerobic exercise a minimum of thirty minutes at a time at least three times a week? ` ___

4. Do you have a set time and schedule to exercise each week? ___

5. Can you jog 1 mile in twelve minutes? If over 55, can you walk 1 mile in twenty minutes? ___

SCORE 1 POINT FOR EVERY **NO** ANSWER BELOW: (QUESTIONS 6-11)

WORK/LIFE **Y / N**

6. Do you eat lunch two or more times each

week at your desk, or do you skip lunch altogether because you're too busy? ___

7. Do you often miss time with your family because work (e-mails, texts, cell phone calls) is interfering? ___

8. Do you worry about your work when you go home at night or on weekends? ___

9. Do you sometimes forego vacation plans because you felt it was more important to get back to work? ___

10. Do you socialize with work associates more than any other people (friends, neighbors?) ___

11. Is your conversation at home and at family functions dominated by your work? ___

SCORE 1 POINT FOR EVERY **YES** ANSWER BELOW: (QUESTIONS 12-17)

INTELLECTUAL AND CULTURAL Y / N

12. Have you attended a concert or live theatre in the past three months? ___

13. Have you visited an art gallery, museum or library in the past three months? ___

14. Have you seen a movie outside your home in the past two months? ___

15. Have you watched an average of less than two hours of TV on the nights you've been home in the past month? ___

16. Have you read a non-work related book in the last month? ___

17. Have you learned something totally new in the past six months (taken a class, learned the stock market, joined Facebook or LinkedIn)? ___

SCORE 1 POINT FOR EVERY **YES** ANSWER BELOW (QUESTION 18-21)

COMMUNITY INVOLVEMENT **Y / N**

18. Are you an active member of a social organization that meets a minimum of ten times a year (country club, book club, social group)? ___

19. Do you participate on a regular basis in an intellectual or service organization (Rotary, Toastmasters, United Way)? ___

20. Are you involved in any volunteer charity work (church, hospital, food bank)? ___

21. Have you become involved in an endeavor that's completely new to you in the last six months? ___

SCORE 1 POINT FOR EVERY **NO** ANSWER BELOW: (QUESTIONS 22-25)

CAREER ACCEPTANCE **Y / N**

22. Do you find yourself unwilling to take on new challenges at the office? ___

23. Do you feel uncomfortable meeting people for the first time? ___

24. Do you often feel bored at work? ___

25. Is the last dare you accepted long since forgotten? ___

TOTAL SCORE ___

MEASURE YOUR RESULTS

25 = Perfect balance!
You know what's important to you, and you attend to the different aspects of your life on a regular basis. It's hard to be perfect all the time. But your awareness and pursuit of this level is outstanding.

21–24 = Very good.

You are well on your way to living a balanced life. Only a few minor adjustments to your life priorities and you're there.

16–20 = Acceptable.

Many people fall into this category. Don't let this be you. I know you want to live a life above this level. Look for ways to improve one category at a time.

13–15 = Needs improvement.

Thanks for being honest with yourself. Now is the time to look at your priorities in life and set targets to improve. Don't put this off any longer. You need to create drastic change in your life or you will never leave this level.

12 or below = It's time to change.

I bet you already know this. You are not a lost cause, but your life probably feels off balance and you're feeling a lot of stress. Set small and achievable goals to get to a higher level within the next sixty days. Don't procrastinate, it's your life your're playing with here.

For additional copies and more information on this Life Planning survey, visit www.PWallin.com

The Purpose Behind the Priorities

PHYSICAL FITNESS

It's not that you have to be a heavy-duty weight lifter, but it's good to be in shape. It gives you energy to make it through your days. If you suffer from the mid-afternoon "drowsies," take a walk and I think you'll find you'll have more energy to carry you through the evening. Practicing good physical fitness habits also boosts your attitude about yourself. Energy begets energy! Finally, once you get your walk or trip to the gym out of the way, you can cross if off the "accomplishment list" because you certainly did something for your health that day!

Personally, I make time to get at least thirty minutes of exercise every day. Sometimes it's simply taking the dogs for a walk. Other times I ride the stationary bike in my living room while watching the Yankees game on TV. And yes, I enjoy playing ice hockey once a week where I not only get a big workout (boy, do I sweat!), but I also have fun playing a game and spending time with my teammates.

WORKAHOLISM

We're all so busy that it's vital to get away from your desk and your routine every once in a while. Don't be afraid to walk away from your computer—it's not going anywhere, and neither are the phone or email messages. Strike a balance and aim not to take work home at night, or, if you work at home, shut off the computer and close the office door. Spend time with your family, spouse, significant other, and pets, and get a good night's rest.

When I started Wallin Insurance, I was working sixty to seventy hours a week, but I made a point of always being home for dinner and to spend some time with my wife and kids. Because I often had evening appointments with insurance prospects I made sure to come home for a little while (the kids were all under the age of 7) and play catch and video games, and to help Marilyn wash the dishes. (Hey, it's my book; this is how I remember those days!)

It's true what they say about balance: It's important to a healthy life, and it makes your productive hours more productive.

INTELLECTUAL AND CULTURAL

Besides getting a break from your work and world, it's good to open your horizons and take in some other worlds too, such as literature, art, or even a movie. It's good for keeping your own mind sharp, and it also provides fodder for intellectual conversations with others.

I'm not much of a museum-goer. I remember as a kid going on a trip to the Henry Ford Museum in Detroit, Michigan, with my parents. I was so grumpy and bored I waited at the exit door while my family toured the museum. It just wasn't for me. But over the years, I've learned to appreciate good culture in the form of live plays and musical performances. Marilyn and I are now season ticket holders at the Clemens Center in Elmira, New York, and have seen outstanding Broadway performances. I must admit, I'm always looking forward to the next show.

COMMUNITY INVOLVEMENT

Community involvement is also good for the soul. Giving your time can turn out to be quite the gift to your community—Little League teams, chambers of commerce, church organizations, and social clubs all need that natural resource for growth. In addition, it expands your centers of influence and friendship base—which could help your career path as well.

I never volunteered for the United Way back when I was a manager in the corporate world. Sure, I donated money (directly from my paycheck), but that was all I did. Once I opened my own business in Elmira, New York, I began to see the need in my local community for leadership. I joined the fundraising cabinet for the local United Way (United Way of the Southern Tier) and over time became leader of this committee. Then, in 2009 I became Chairman of the Board. Not only is this a huge honor, but I feel I am now in position to showcase my talents and develop future leaders among my local contacts to help this organization for years to come.

It's not about fame or recognition. I'm not telling you this to impress you. Rather, I'm telling you this to impress upon you that you should strongly consider getting further involved in your community.

CAREER ACCEPTANCE

I think you've got to enjoy what you're doing—even if you don't want to be doing it forever. There's a reason people sometimes refer to jobs as "making a living." We spend, proportionally, much of our lives at work. That time should be fulfilling. You owe that much to yourself.

Find ways to be the absolute best at the job you're given today and good things will happen. You'll get noticed by your current employer—or another one who wants you to bring your enthusiasm to his or her office. Be committed to your existing job, while remaining open to new things. Also, remember to take a dare once in a while. Take a chance on something new such as a big assignment, even if it creates more work for you. *That's the formula for advancement.*

Today my life is the best it's ever been. I enjoy each and every moment, whether I'm at work, on the road or at home with my family. I have less stress in my life and have more control over my schedule and my priorities.

Your life can be improved too, when you ask yourself, **"How can I make my current situation better?"** Use this Life Balance tool on a regular basis, perhaps once a month, to gauge your personal growth.

Your answers will create your true identity, and assist you on your journey toward living your dream.

LIVING THE DREAM

Challenge yourself to live a properly balanced life. This will be your guide in your quest toward self-improvement and lifelong happiness.

Chapter 2

LIVE IN THE MOMENT

"Life is what happens to you when you're busy making other plans."

JOHN LENNON
(1940-1980) MUSICIAN, SONG-WRITER AND PEACE ACTIVIST

I used to get so wrapped up in worrying about my past or planning my future that I rarely paid attention to what was happening around me. We all have the tendency to know what we need to do, but we get overwhelmed by the events around us. We lose focus.

That's why it's imperative to live in the present—right here, right now!

Marv Levy, former coach of my beloved Buffalo Bills, took his team to the Super Bowl an unprecedented four years in a row back in the early 1990s. During that run, he became known in the football circles for his motivational pre-game rallies. "This is our team, this is our time," he'd exclaim. "Where would you rather be than right here, right now?" The players adored their coach, and appreciated his colorful vocabulary and genuine attitude toward the game. His big words were all they needed to get focused on the job at hand—namely, their opponent.

Levy's teams learned to play one game at a time, rather than thinking about what happened in last week's game or might happen in next week's. Instead, the center of attention was lasered on the only game that mattered: today's. The Buffalo Bills earned a trip to four straight Super Bowls, and, even thought they lost, it was their perseverance and crisp focus that kept bringing them back.

It's tempting for many of us to look back at our own days past. Some want to reclaim high school glories or punish themselves with regrets. People who live like this are wrecking their minds and their bodies. Their focus on a past that no longer exists is preventing them from seeing the possibilities of real relationships right in front of them.

It's great to remember those moments in life where you got your driver's license or kissed a girl for the first time, but it's unhealthy to get stuck there. In worst-case scenarios, experts suggest that those who are chronically disconnected from the present may even experience depression or develop self-destructive habits.

LIVING THE DREAM

When memories exceed dreams, we are in trouble. The key to happiness is to live in the moment.

Happiness begins with having the right feeling about yourself and who you are. It's a feeling of wholeness, of confidence in your abilities, and of support from the important people in your life.

SALUTATION TO THE DAWN

Each day when I wake up I recite the Salutation to the Dawn. I have it pasted to my bathroom mirror—even though I know it by heart. It's a reminder to myself of how I need to live the day ahead.

The Salutation was written hundreds of years ago by Kaldasa, an Indian dramatist. These enduring words are as relevant today as ever. Rewrite it in your best penmanship and tape it to your bathroom mirror. This first thing you see in the morning will inspire you to remember to live for this day only.

SALUTATION TO THE DAWN

Look to this Day!
For it is life, the very life of life
In its brief course
Lie all the verities and realities of your existence
The bliss of growth
The glory of action
The splendor of beauty,
For yesterday is but a dream
And tomorrow is only a vision,
But today well lived makes every dream of yesterday
a dream of happiness
And every tomorrow a vision of hope
Look well, therefore to this day!
such is the salutation to the dawn

My life has changed a lot as I've gotten older. I've learned to appreciate things each and every day. I look at every meal as if it were a banquet and every activity as if it were a parade. I now take time with my kids—sometimes we do things as a family, sometimes we do things one-on-one:

- Once a year my oldest son, Mike, along with my brother, Mike, embark on a sports weekend trip. We travel to a select location (after careful evaluation of the sports calendar) to attend football, hockey, or another sporting event. We've been to Miami, Tampa, Baltimore, Washington, DC, and Arizona. I can't wait to see where we end up heading this year!

- My son Pete and I just finished visiting colleges. In my mind, it doesn't really matter which college he decides to attend. What was important for us at this time was to spend some quality time together discussing his future and how I can support him and his dreams.

- And Angela—my only daughter—just loves shopping in Chinatown in New York City. While it's truly a remarkable place, what sticks with me is the experience we get to share together. It's more than worth it (as long as she goes easy on my credit card!). We've also begun an annual camping trip to Darien Lake where she and her friends attend an all-day outdoor concert while I stay at the campground thinking about the next chapter in my upcoming book. We meet up each night for a campfire.

LIVING THE DREAM

"Decide upon your major definite purpose in life and then organize all of your activities around it."

BRIAN TRACY

SELF-HELP AUTHOR AND SPEAKER

Tim Russert was the author of the book *Wisdom of Our Fathers* (Random House 2007). Not only was he an avid Buffalo Bills fan himself, he also understood the importance of spending time with loved ones:

"It has been said a million times, but it's so true: Time is the most precious commodity of all. You can shower a child with presents or money, but what do they really mean, compared to the most valuable gift of all – your time? Your time together doesn't have to be programmed or planned. Vacations and special events are nice, but so often the best moments are the spontaneous ones when nothing much is happening. Every moment you spend with your loved ones could be the one that really matters."

Russert passed away (after suffering a heart attack at the age of 58), a short time after he released this book. But you can tell he had his priorities in line as he shared his love for his son, Luke, as well as the rest of his family.

It's sometimes hard to live in the moment. Personally, I used to get distracted and let self-doubt get in the way. Things I've been afraid of in the past—like taking a day off of work—caused me a lot of stress. I would feel guilty when I spent time with my family when I thought I should be working. I would often let my work take over for the really important things in life. My work had become an easy excuse for not doing what really mattered.

I think there's a fear that exists in each of us that tends to hold us back from doing the things we really want to do. Fear of being replaced at work. Fear of taking on a new challenge (because we might fail). Fear of calling someone we haven't talked to in a while because the last time there was an unpleasant encounter.

OVERCOMING FEAR

Fear has a way of creeping up on us . Are you afraid to take a day off of work? Are you afraid to commit to a relationship? Afraid to ask for a raise, afraid of not making a sale, or afraid to confront your boss or co-worker? It seems that almost all of our fears are self-created. We frighten ourselves into thinking that bad things will happen to us if we venture out of our comfort zone. Well, let's tackle this issue.

In my opinion **fear** stands for:

FALSE
EVIDENCE THAT
APPEARS
REAL.

That's right. Most of the things we fear or worry about never happen. They may seem real on the surface, but I've often said that most of all the bad things we worry about (I'd say about 98%) never occur. It's all in our minds. We agonize about things and ultimately begin to feel pain in our stomach. It's not so much the fact that a bad thing might happen. Some things in life we cannot control. I believe it's the actual **fear** that causes the most harm to us.

Humorist Mark Twain once said, *"I have lived a long life and had many troubles, most of which never happened."*

When I first entered the sales world I was a shy and nervous kid. Even though I was 25 years old I looked about 17. I was concerned about being professional and competent enough to be able to talk to a person about his or her insurance, especially life insurance, which was often a major decision in people's lives. Many of my prospects were older and more established in their home lives and careers than I was. My worry caused sleepless nights and an uneasy stomach.

I soon learned a magic formula from studying Dale Carnegie's *How to Stop Worrying and Start Living* (Simon and Schuster, 1984). It truly helped me overcome this issue and help me become a good salesperson. If you have a worry problem, apply the following formula by doing these three things:

1. Ask yourself, "What's the worst that can possibly happen?"
2. Prepare to accept it if you have to.
3. Then calmly proceed to improve on the worst.

So, here's what I did. I first asked myself, "What's the worst that can happen?" Well, if I didn't make a sale I would still be alive, my wife Marilyn would still love me, and the potential client probably wouldn't pull a gun on me. I can accept that. No big deal. I then began to calmly do the things I knew I needed to do to improve this situation—like get training on the proper insurance product and developing solid people skills to be able to ask the prospect the right questions so I could begin to solve his or her problem. And if this particular person decided not to buy my product, I would learn from my experience and find someone else to talk to.

The results were magical. I immediately eliminated the worry and stress in my life and began to help myself by helping others. I realized that I loved my job, the insurance business. I enjoyed the fact that I could help myself (earn commissions) by helping others (secure their insurance).

Now over two decades later, I can honestly say this magical formula transformed my life. Yes, stress will always exist in one form or another. But I know how to control it and build from it.

IT'S TIME TO STOP WORRYING AND START LIVING

Once stress is recognized, I suggest using this magical formula and busting out of a negative mind set. Learn to create a series of little victories in your everyday life. Begin focusing on stress management activities that don't necessarily require a lot of effort. Minor adjustments can go a long way toward living in the present moment. Here's a few ideas:

1) **Take a daily walk.** Perhaps with your dog and your iPod. In addition to getting a bit of exercise you will free up your mind from the activities of your workday and allow you to focus on the beauty that surrounds you. Enjoy exploring new places as well as feeling good about yourself for getting some exercise.

2) **Pick up a hammer.** I've often found that when I'm working on a home remodeling project I enjoy the physical aspect of the job. I don't get a chance to construct thing with my hands while at work (the keyboard doesn't count), so when I am building things at home I lose all the fears and stresses of my everyday life because I'm concentrating so much on the task at hand. Marilyn and I often do these projects together—it's that quality time together—and it's cheaper than taking her on a vacation. In all honesty I'm pretty good at breaking things apart, like knocking down a wall, but not so good at putting things back together. But who really cares? I'm simply trying to eliminate my stress!

   Mark Twain also said, *"To be busy is man's only happiness."* Well, I'm not sure if this is my only happiness, but I do enjoy working with my hands.

3) **Appreciate those closest to you**. Spend quality time with your spouse, your children, your brothers and sisters, and your best friends. Make gratitude a frequent attitude. Time with them is more important than anything else in the world, even if it's not a lot of time. Make it a point to eat dinner together at home or go to a local restaurant, and take that time to catch up with each other and chat about what happened at school or work. There's magic that happens when you really start listening and sharing the little things that go on in your day. I'm sure you'll find yourself laughing over something funny or

sharing stories about something that happened during the day, or planning upcoming activities.

4) **Stay fresh**—go to bed thirty minutes earlier at night. It's amazing how refreshed you will feel in the morning after a good night's sleep. The average adult person now only gets 6.7 hours of sleep each night. I like my eight hours! You won't have trouble getting up and getting ready for the day when you've registered a good night's rest. Reading a good book before bedtime may help you sleep better, and turn off the TV!

5) **Take a nap**—even if you do get a good night's rest, know that rest is repair. There is so much repair that even a twenty-minute afternoon "power nap" will give you. Famous people like Winston Churchill, Eleanor Roosevelt and Thomas Edison have all attributed having enormous energy and endurance to their habit of sleeping a bit during the day. I've been doing this myself for years as well. And I can tell you that the "rest before you are tired" philosophy doesn't cure fatigue, it prevents it.

6) **Build some personal time into your schedule.** Carry a "to-do" list of things you need to accomplish each day, or type it into your BlackBerry. Add one or two items like "go to the library" or "read my hometown newspaper online." These activities, even if they only take 15 minutes, will give you some quiet time and allow you to break up

your day and refresh yourself before tackling another chore on your list.

7) **Call a friend.** Nourish the friendships in your life. Make it a daily habit to talk to three people face to face or on the phone. It's easy to send e-mails and text messages, but emotional contact is diminished. Good ol'-fashioned conversation strengthens relationships and you'll certainly be liked and respected for taking time to call.

8) **Plan a trip,** whether it be a family vacation or a reunion with school friends. Every year my college buddies from Binghamton University and I plan a get-together. For several weeks leading up to our fall weekend we call and e-mail each other as we plan our next adventure. It takes a bit of coordination as we arrange our travel itinerary (we choose a different venue each year). But I must say that the planning of this journey is just as fun as the destination itself. I've learned that when there's something to look forward to in life, there's a little more in the jump of my step in the days and weeks leading up to the event itself. So, I always have my next trip in mind.

9) **Take the Life Balance survey again.** Look at each of the 25 questions. (See Chapter 1.) What areas are you already good at? What areas need improvement? Set a goal to improve your score—and set a deadline to actually accomplish it.

10) Say the *Serenity Prayer*—the best 27-words of advice I know:

God grant me the serenity
To accept the things I cannot change,
The courage to change the things I can;
And the wisdom to know the difference.

LIVING THE DREAM

"Live today as if this were the last day of your life, because one day, you will be right!"

Chapter 3

BE WHERE YOU ARE WHEN YOU'RE THERE

"It is what we learn after we think we know it all, that counts."

TONY ROBBINS
AMERICAN SELF-HELP WRITER,
SPEAKER AND MOTIVATOR

I was attending a business seminar a few years ago when I heard the speaker say: BE WHERE YOU ARE WHEN YOU'RE THERE.

"Okay," I said to myself. "What does that mean? Of course I know where I am, I'm here in this conference room listening to this speaker. What on earth is this message all about?"

After pondering this thought for a few moments with confusion and bewilderment, I began to get the message. Even though I was at this meeting, my mind was wandering. Like most of my days, it was a busy one, and I was thinking about all the things that needed to be done, such as making some important phone calls, checking my e-mail, and attending two more meetings with customers before going home to Marilyn and the kids. I had a lot on my mind, but I was confident in myself to complete all of these tasks, because I was good at that. I knew how to get my tasks done, and I was proud of myself.

"BE WHERE YOU ARE WHEN YOU'RE THERE." Really!

TO DO TODAY

I suggest you read the following when you rise every morning. It will get you focused on the important things you should do and put you in the right frame of mind—for when you are excited and cheerful about the upcoming day, unbelievable things can happen.

- **Today I will be happy.** I know that I become what I think about. So if I think happy and positive thoughts, I will be a happy and positive person. By doing this I will feel great—both inside and out.

- **Today I will accept the things I can control** and not worry about the things I cannot control. Doing this will reduce the stress in my life.

- **Today I will strengthen my mind.** I will read a minimum of one hour and challenge myself to learn something new. Doing this will improve my mental concentration and knowledge about a variety of things.

- **Today I will do something physical.** I will exercise, take a walk, or go to the gym. Doing this will make me feel energized and fit.

- **Today I will live in day-tight compartments**. I will concentrate first on the most important things that need to be done today, and, if there's time, I'll tackle the not-so-important issues. This will show me how to set priorities and form habits of getting things done.

- **Today I will meet three new people.** Doing this will expand my social life, my business life, and my personal life.

- **Today I will do something with my family and close friends.** Doing this will build memories that will be remembered for the rest of my life. It's not about the places I visit; it's about the people I visit.

- **Today I will do something for my community.** This will not only benefit others but will teach me the importance of sharing my time, talent and treasures.

- **Today I will be unafraid to try something new.** If I fail, I understand it's just a learning opportunity. Doing this will teach me to be willing to take a risk.

- **Today I will relax.** I will take some quiet time by myself and think about what is important to me, and say a little prayer of thanks for all the gifts I've been given. Doing this will make me feel good about myself and my life.

BE WHERE YOU ARE

To be engaged in your current activities, you must learn to live in "day-tight compartments." Live one day at a time, with no worries about the past and no concerns about the future. Simply focus on having a clear picture of what's right in front of you.

If you're at work, be at work.

If you're at home, be at home.

If you're at the gym, be at the gym.

If you're at your child's soccer game, be at the soccer game.

I recently played in an ice hockey game for my team, the "Iceaholics." My son Mike was on our team as well. (We have a mix of young adults and older veterans playing together.) We played offense together on the same line. We were so focused and "in the zone" playing together we actually combined to score five goals in the first period of the game. We seemed to know where to pass to and where each other would be positioned. The other team and their goalie had no chance. I truly savored the opportunity to play with Mike and have some fun. We were totally focused.

You get the point? If your body is there, then let your mind be there. Don't get caught up in distractions—especially that phone call or that text that's waiting for you; those can wait. Be in the present moment now and when it's time to check the messages, be in the present moment then. Trust me: Not being "on alert" for the email or text message will immediately make you relax more. And, yes, when emergencies arise, certainly it's important to take the call. But how often does that happen? There really aren't many emergencies if you have planned your day appropriately.

LIVING THE DREAM

Lack of planning on someone else's part should not constitute an emergency on my part.

THE CELL PHONE DILEMMA

I recently went to a large mall on a shopping excursion with my teenage daughter, Angela. While following her from store to store (I was in charge of carrying the bags), I couldn't help but notice many of the patrons using their cell phones, some talking, many sending texts. They were staring at the screens and punching away at the keyboard. Some were walking down the aisles actually bumping into other cell phone users—both parties too engulfed in their own world, not paying attention to what was going on around them.

I truly believe the cellular telephone has become the most amazing invention of all time. Yes, of all time! More than any other invention in the world including electricity, the automobile, or the space shuttle. This device allows people to communicate with each other no matter where we are or what we are doing. It is incredible!

But in many ways it has overtaken us. The cell phone user is now very open in public, either talking, texting, or browsing the Internet, while the people around them are ignored.

Yes, it's happened to me as well, where all five of us go to dinner in a restaurant and all five of us are engrossed in our own personal device world that we're not aware of what's going on at our own dinner table. I must admit it's kind of funny but in reality it's a wasted opportunity. As my teenagers become more and more busy with their own lives—school, sports, work, and friends—we often don't get a chance to gather as a family. So, we've adopted rules where there's no cell usage while we're together for a meal. Most of the time we abide by this rule (that includes me!). We now can concentrate on good old-fashioned conversation. And I must admit I truly enjoy these times we spend together.

BE ATTENTIVE

Success is the sum of small efforts, repeated day in and day out. You don't have to create a masterpiece; just turn your focus to the things right in front of you.

- When you're in your office having a scheduled meeting with a co-worker, you should not answer the phone when it rings. You should not be staring at your computer to see the latest e-mail that just hit your inbox. Rather, give the other person 100 percent of your undivided attention.
- When you're at the soccer field, pay attention to the game and watch each play. That way you can have a real conversation with your child after the game and share what the game looked like from your vantage point.
- When you're out on a date with your spouse or significant other, make sure you are listening attentively and paying attention. He or she will notice how well you are responding to him or her and don't be surprised when you both realize you have had a great time.

LIVING THE DREAM

Life is simply a handful of short stories pretending to be a novel. Make it a best seller! Cherish each moment you have with your friends and loved ones.

Chapter 4

TAKE A CHANCE

"I have three treasures.
Guard and keep them:
The first is deep love,
The second is frugality,
And the third is not to dare to be ahead
of the world.
Because of deep love, one is courageous.
Because of frugality, one is generous.
Because of not daring to be ahead
of the world, one becomes the leader
of the world."

WARREN BUFFETT
INVESTOR, BUSINESSMAN AND PHILANTHROPIST

What does the above statement mean? Does it mean that we shouldn't take a chance? As I write this chapter I really thought long and hard about what Warren Buffett is saying. For a time I even thought about eliminating it, because initially it didn't make sense to me. What do you mean "don't be ahead of the world"? Isn't that what you've done? Come on, Mr. Buffett, share your coveted secrets with us!

But the quote kept nagging at me and now I think I get it. In a nutshell, having love in your life is critical. That's where happiness begins, and ultimately lasts forever. That's where we've all heard, *"It's wonderful to have loved and lost than not to have loved at all."* Being **frugal** with your money allows you to reduce the stresses of life that exist when there's too much debt, credit card problems and high interest rates. Many people I know always seem to have a cloud over their head—they just can't seem to get ahead. **Not daring to be ahead** of the world simply means we should learn from the successes of others. Trying new and unproven ideas can often bring frustrating results, and no return on capital. But learning from experiences is what allows us to mature into well-rounded people with valuable insights.

This chapter is dedicated to analyzing Buffet's quote even more deeply. I'll break it down line by line and offer my feelings and opinions. In the end, I believe you'll understand how you can better live your own life.

DEEP LOVE

Yep, this one is pretty easy. I have anecdotes sprinkled throughout this entire book about love. It must be worked at; it must be cherished. Once we have achieved the feeling of deep love it is easy to have courage:

- Courage to say "I love you" out loud. I learned this one

from my brother, Mike. He's the baby of our big family (even though he's now in his 40s) Over the years, Mike has engaged us all in showing us how to hug each other and actually say the words every time we talk to each other. Since our family is scattered across the country, we are lucky if we all get together two or three times a year. But, when we do, we take the time to affectionately embrace and show our love. We didn't always do this growing up, but now we are open with our feelings. I think it is a direct result of our family experiences with illness and death, and the fact that we don't get to physically see each other very often. At first it felt a bit uncomfortable, but now the words flow because we all know how important it is to not just feel it, but to say it.

"None of us can change our yesterdays, but all of us can change our tomorrows."

COLIN POWELL,
RETIRED U.S. SECRETARY OF STATE

- Courage to be honest. Because of deep love, there's no holding back. Telling each other our candid feelings through straight-talk keeps us all on the same page. That's what I love about my wife, Marilyn. She'll always tell me what's on her mind. There's no need for me to interpret her feelings. She tells me!
- Doing the "little things." Simple gestures like cleaning the kitchen, taking out the trash, or doing a load of laundry (without being asked) are all signs of love.

Somehow I think Marilyn likes this more than when I buy her a bouquet of flowers.

- Sending a card. My sister Mary and I have our birthdays two days apart in August. Hers is the 15th, mine is the 17th. One year I mailed her a corny card with a Buffalo Bills football logo on the cover. As soon as she received it she immediately signed HER name to it and mailed it right back to me. She recycled it. How dare she do that! Well, that immediately set off a run where our entire family now sends recycled cards to each other. Some of the cards (I think there's three or four of them in circulation) are over ten years old. It's fun to look at them now, filled with signatures and dates from birthdays past. It's a little tradition, but it's truly a statement of love.

FRUGALITY

I could probably write a whole other book on this topic, but for now I'll say this:

Living a debt-free life has become the new definition of wealth. No longer is it considered impressive to drive a Mercedes; it's now impressive to be free of debt.

Dave Ramsey, author of the book *Total Money Makeover* (Thomas Nelson Inc. 2007) has become one of the most recognizable financial gurus of this era. He has a weekly show on cable news networks where he recognizes callers who declare they have officially cut up their credit cards. He says that "the number one rule to wealth is to not have monthly installment payments." I know this isn't easy for many people, but it's worthy of setting goals to reduce or eliminate monthly balances on credit cards.

Learning to live within your means is sometimes not easy. We all want the newest iPod, the latest cell phone, or the 42-inch plasma TV. But it shouldn't be purchased if it cannot be afforded. Running up credit cards applies pressure to the household finances, and ultimately causes stress and family friction. Live a thrifty life and don't get into trouble buying things you cannot afford.

I am currently in the process of helping my three teenage kids to understand this. Buying with a credit card is unacceptable (unless it's a true emergency); using a debit card is the key, because you have to have the money in your bank account to buy something. "Act your wage," I tell them. "Your money is 20 percent knowledge and 80 percent behavior."

Mr. Buffett himself still lives in the same moderate house he moved into in 1958. He paid just $31,500 for it. A reporter from *The Oregonian* recently wrote that as he drove by the house one day he saw a clothes line hanging in the yard. Buffett's purpose in life is not to show off to impress the neighbors. His purpose is to be financially smart and be philanthropic in his gestures. We can all learn something from that.

DON'T BE AHEAD OF THE WORLD

Taking chances promotes personal growth and builds experience. But it should be done only after taking valuable education from others and preparing yourself for success, not failure. I have filled my life with taking chances and being brave. I've done things such as skydiving, hitchhiking across the country, and quitting my successful job to start my own business when I had three children under the age of 7. But I learned early on the importance of proper training and planning before taking that leap. I couldn't simply trust the parachute to open from 10,000 feet without testing the equipment before the jump.

TAKE CALCULATED RISKS

Risks should be carefully thought out. You don't need to do things that have never been done before. Rather, do things that YOU have never done before. When I wrote my first book I didn't try to invent a whole new category to have my book stand all by itself on the shelf at Borders or Barnes & Noble bookstores. Instead, I went to those places and saw what books were already on display in my category. Authors such as Dr. Stephen Covey, Napoleon Hill, and Jeffrey Gitomer had popular books already published in the field of marketing and business. I then set a goal to one day have my finished book sit right alongside these successful authors. (Thankfully, I achieved that goal. It's cool now to go to my local Barnes & Noble bookstore and see my book on the shelf right next to Tony Robbins's books.)

"There is a difference between being interested and being committed. When you're interested in doing something, you do it only when it's convenient. When you're committed to something, you accept no excuses, only results."

KEN BLANCHARD, AUTHOR OF OVER THIRTY BOOKS, INCLUDING *THE ONE MINUTE MANAGER*.

RISKS BRING GROWTH

By stretching yourself a little bit more each time, you are conditioning yourself for long-lasting development. Take a class; read books regularly; try new things that interest and intrigue you. You will grow with a constant and never-ending approach.

IMAGINE YOURSELF ALREADY AT THE PEAK

By visualizing your positive outcome you are training your brain that success is imminent. Andre Agassi, a former number-one world tennis player and winner of eight Grand Slam events, was once asked how special it felt to win the U.S. Open. He said, "I knew the feeling. I had been there at the winner's circle many times holding the trophy. I dreamt about it for years. When it finally happened I knew how to react, because I had already been there."

BE ORIGINAL

I gave a speech several years ago about "8 Steps to Character Development." (See www.Pwallin.com.) In Agassi's style I said: "I've given this speech so many times in this past decade; I know it so well. But this is the first time I've given it in front of an audience." I had memorized this speech and lived the concepts for almost a decade. So when I finally got the chance to share it with others, the words just flowed naturally. I felt very natural and confident.

I promised myself I wouldn't use analogies in this book like "re-inventing the wheel," "that's the best idea since sliced bread," or "you don't need to be a rocket scientist." Those cliches slip off our tongues so easily these days we tend to forget their meaning. What I believe is this: It's not critical that you re-invent something. Rather, it's important that you "be yourself." Live within your means but continue to **explore, dream, and discover** what opportunities exist in the world for you. Be willing to take a chance and try things that will make you grow more as a person.

IT'S OKAY TO TAKE CALCULATED RISKS

Are you willing to accept a dare? Do you remember the last time you were afraid to try something? These questions are a part of the **Life Balance** survey from chapter one. How did you answer them?

My mother, now in her 80s, is still an active person mentally and physically. She has learned to keep her mind fresh by reading as much as she possibly can. For a lady who never attended college, she can probably beat 99 percent of everyone who plays Jeopardy on television. She has a quote from Eleanor Roosevelt hanging on her refrigerator door: *"Do something every day that scares you."* I'm not going to force you into being scared every day for the rest of your life, but I am going to ask you to consider stretching yourself a little more.

Trying something new each day (call it a "TSNED") will bring a new sense of experience that will help you overcome dull and boring days. Trying new things will allow you to grow in areas of love, relationships, family, money, and contribution to your community.

Back in our college years, my sisters, Mary and Linda, and I used to play a game of "TSNED." It was often simple things such as going up and talking to a stranger in the grocery store line or driving a new route through the state of New York to get to my college in Binghamton or Mary's home at Cornell University in Ithaca. We had fun challenging each other to get out of our comfort zone and create new experiences we all could learn from. Even the simplest of things—as long as we've never done them before—counted in our game. We went to new restaurants together and tried new variety of beers (we were in college, after all!), and my sisters even taught me how to do laundry. We turned our game into experiences that made us stronger and more confident—a "been there, done that" attitude.

EXPLORE

The most common mistake people make when trying to create more happiness in their lives is playing it too safe. By limiting and confining activities to only those things with guaranteed success, it's actually setting the person up for disappointment. It makes life too predictable and too complacent.

Life needs to be revitalized! Look for new and creative things to bring excitement to it! Be willing to expand your comfort zone and mindful of opportunities that will bring levels of happiness to you never before dreamed of.

Because of deep love, one is courageous.
Because of frugality, one is generous.
Because of not daring to be ahead of the world,
one becomes leader of the world.

Read these words again. Let them sink in. Make them become a part of your life from now on. It works for Warren Buffett, one of the richest people on this planet, it can also work for you.

LIVING THE DREAM

Take a chance, learn something valuable every day. Live it, feel it, enjoy it...and savor it. Then share it with someone else.

Chapter 5

LIVING ON CLOUD 9

"Life would be infinitely happier if we could be born at the age of eighty and gradually approach eighteen."

MARK TWAIN
(1835-1910) AMERICAN AUTHOR AND HUMORIST

In my speeches I frequently talk about the importance of being happy. I explain the significance of living in the moment and keeping focused on the top priorities in life. In one of my points I say, "You become what you think about. If you think positive thoughts, you will be a positive person. If you think negative thoughts, you will be a negative person. It's that simple."

One time after delivering this speech, a member of the audience asked, "You are so enthusiastic. How do you remain so upbeat and positive?"

Well, in truth no one can be happy and positive all the time. Not even me. I experience my share of sadness, frustration, anger, discomfort, and impatience (especially when

I'm driving!). But I don't dwell on it. I have developed the ability to be hyper-aware of this condition, and I immediately look for a way to snap out of it. How do I do this? Well, I take a walk, or begin a new remodeling project at home, or simply sit in silence and think about what is happening to me and how I can deal with it. I concentrate on what happened to make me feel this way. I look for the origin and I take measures to change my feelings toward the situation. I ask myself, "What have I learned here? How can this make me a stronger person?"

In all honesty, I believe I am a very blessed person. I say a prayer of thanks each and every day for good health, a happy family, a meaningful career, and a sharp mind to make wise decisions. It hasn't always been easy. I've had my share of failures and setbacks—like not getting a job promotion, missing out on the big sale, or missing my son's big goal at the soccer game. But I've learned from these experiences.

Michael Jordan, one of the greatest basketball players who ever played, once said: "I've missed more than 9,000 shots in my career. I've lost almost 300 games. Twenty-six times I've been trusted to take the game winning shot and missed. I've failed over and over and over again in my life and that is why I succeed." Now that's confidence! Having the attitude that you will always take something away from a bad experience can be very healthy and rewarding. Instead of dwelling on the negative, take something positive that will help you the next time you're in a position of further shaping your destiny.

THE CLOUDS AND THE SUN

Some people always seem to have dark clouds hanging over them. Clouds tend to represent bad things—gloom and doom (except if you're on "Cloud 9"). For these people, something is always going wrong. They just can't seem to get out of debt, they can't lose the weight they want to lose, or they can't get the career break they're looking for. Now I know we are living in a difficult time, the economy is struggling and unemployment rate is at double-digit levels, but check out the following statistics:

The **divorce rate** in our country is very high. The National Center for Health Statistics recently released a report which found that 43 percent of first marriages end in separation or divorce within fifteen years.

The **obesity rate** in America is astounding. According to the Centers for Disease Control and Prevention, currently about 31 percent, or about 59 million people, are obese, which is defined as roughly 30 or more pounds over a healthy weight. That's up from 12% in 1990. By the year 2020 this trend is expected to grow to 40% or more.

The **retirement savings rate** is weak. At a time when Americans are living longer, more than half the paid workers ages 25 to 64 don't own retirement savings accounts of any kind. With an up-and-down economy and employers cutting jobs, this is an alarming statistic.

I don't mean to get you down with these sour statistics; stick with me here. My concern is that there's a lot of bad stuff happening in our world. And many people are caught up in it. It causes low self-esteem, depression, and discomfort in social situations. It just seems as if there's a dark cloud hanging over some people, and it tends to drag everything and everyone down around you.

But it can be overcome! It's time to find Cloud 9.

I've often said, "It's not what happens to you, it's how you respond to what happens to you." Sometimes you'll have a knee-jerk reaction to something, like when they don't accept your offer to buy a certain home. Initially you may react by saying, "I really liked that home. Why is this happening to me?" But after you settle down and think about it, wouldn't it be great to have a response like: "It's no big deal. I guess this really wasn't meant to be. I'll probably find an even nicer house." Everything happens for a reason, and by having faith in God and your own abilities to complete a task and overcome an obstacle in a positive manner, you will grow by leaps and bounds.

That's what I mean. Have a positive attitude, and see the sun through the clouds.

People are happiest when they have done something— however big or small— they originally considered a challenge. Happy people do this all the time. Unhappy people are not willing to take risks or try something that would make them uncomfortable. But that's where growth and experience comes from.

OVERCOMING FAILURE

When my daughter, Angela, was in seventh grade she tried out for the girls' soccer team. There was a lot of competition during the first few days of practice—in the scorching heat. At the end of the week of tryouts the coach had a meeting with each kid. When it came to Angela's turn, she was told she did not make the team. She was told that she was not fast enough and that her ball dribbling skills were below par. She had a great attitude but it just wasn't enough.

Angela was devastated. She wanted to make this team and be with her classmates. I tried everything I could to console her, but nothing worked (until I promised to buy her a new puppy, but that's a different story).

Instead of giving up the sport completely Angela did a couple of things that made me proud. She began running on her own several times a week in an attempt to improve her speed and get in better shape. She also went to the soccer games and watched as the players passed the ball, trapped the ball, and dribbled. She kept her emotions in check and built a determination that she would make the team the following year.

Sure enough, the next season she earned a spot on the roster, and was actually one of the best players. The coach remarked at her big improvement, and she became one of the leaders of the team. She learned the role of sweeper on defense and the team went undefeated. In subsequent years she tried out for the JV team as she entered high school and was selected as a captain. As I write this book she is now a member of the varsity team and is playing very well. She progressed to the role of leader and communicator out there on the field. She no longer feels resentment for being cut back in her younger days. Instead, she feels a sense of satisfaction that she overcame her failure (in her mind it was only temporary), and is now in control of her destiny.

Bottom line: She is now a stronger person for having faced adversity (at a young age) and not giving up.

REACT VS. RESPONSE

It's easy to be negative and unmotivated. And there's always someone you can blame for something that goes wrong. But it takes hard work to be positive and motivated. You will become a stronger person by learning from your setbacks and having the determination to succeed. I've often said it's not important how you react to what happens to you. Rather, it's important how you respond—after completely understanding your situation and determining your next steps of action. It is in these response stages of your life that your true character is revealed.

SKUNKED

My wife, Marilyn, and I came home late one night after seeing a show. I let our two West Highland Terriers outside to do their business. As I stood at the door I heard them barking out in the distance and peered into the pitch dark to see what the commotion was all about. Then I called their names, and they came running back toward the house. Before I realized it, they were in the house, and the smell was overpowering. Yep, they'd been skunked. "Yikes," I screamed. "We're in trouble." The dogs were running throughout the house, leaving a pungent smell everywhere they went.

Marilyn immediately got them back outside, while I raced to the computer. I searched online about how to eliminate skunk odor on a dog and had my choice of responses. Instead of panicking, we took the advice provided by the click of a mouse and followed the directions. We combined hydrogen peroxide, baking soda, and dishwashing soap, put it on the dogs for 10 minutes, and then thoroughly washed them with warm water. It worked! The smell was gone. The inside of the house smelled for a few days afterward, but, overall, problem easily solved.

LIVING THE DREAM

It's not what happens to you. It's how you respond to what happens that creates your identity.

Instead of panicking or complaining about this disaster, we immediately took action and found a remedy to our problem. It turned out to be no big deal. Plus, we now know, through experience, how to deal with a situation like this the next time we are confronted by it (and thank goodness for Google!).

We've told this story to many people. Step by step we retraced our steps with this experience. Sure, it wasn't funny, but we didn't panic or complain either. Now, we can look and laugh a bit, we have a story to tell. And we usually tell it with a big smiles on our faces – because we overcame a disaster and accomplished something. Marilyn and I are certainly mindful of the fact that no one got hurt, the smell on the dogs eventually went away, and we returned to normal after a few days. We dwell on the positive and forget the negative.

BE DETERMINED

In many ways, it's not a good idea to make constant happiness your ultimate goal. You don't want to place such high expectations for yourself. Instead, focus on doing things in your life that will bring you the feelings you desire—feelings of growth, courage, passion, and joy.

Pursuing happiness is a journey, not a destination. It's like planning for a vacation. The preparation and planning are half the fun. The feeling of anticipation makes you sleep better and have a little more spring in your step when you're awake. I believe we should strive to feel like this every day, not just when we're planning a trip.

Spend time each day asking yourself the following:

- What must I do to enjoy my day today?
- Who do I need to talk to so I get what I want?
- Who can I help get what they want?

- Where should I go to get answers to my questions?
- How can I measure my success?

When you feel good about your answers and know you have the ability to control your situation you will know you have arrived on Cloud 9. What is Cloud 9? It's a feeling of total happiness and bliss—and you control every aspect of it.

We all have within our own hands the ability to fashion our own destiny. With a focus on proper life balance, living in the moment, and striving to reach our peak potential, we will have sharpened these tools. Cloud 9 is no longer just a dream, it is reality. And it can be achieved.

It will take 100 percent effort to remain focused. Share your thoughts and goals with the important people in your life. Be open and honest and take critical feedback as needed. Pray to God to give you these gifts you truly desire so you can go forth to show others who you really are. Touch the world in ways you could never before have imagined.

Go forth and pursue your own Cloud 9!

LIVING THE DREAM

What you become and how you respond to things that happen in your life is the greatest part about living on Cloud 9.
It's not a place; it's a feeling.

Chapter 6

REACHING THE PEAK

"The realm of possibility already exists inside each of us."

PETER WALLIN
AUTHOR AND BUSINESSMAN

There clearly is a high point that can be reached in the world of happiness and living a positive life. By focusing on what's right instead of what's wrong and following a clear set of progressions, you can achieve this lifetime of happiness I've been talking about. It starts with setting goals, and once they're achieved, you then have the ability to advance to a higher stage.

Abraham Maslow has been called the pioneer of positive psychology. He used a pyramid to describe the levels of natural human needs and growth. He called it the "hierarchy of needs." When needs at one level are met, a person naturally progresses to the nest level.

It is here that I have found a better understanding about the important things in life. I have come to learn that

I can control a lot of what is around me, while not worrying about the things I cannot control. By having a clear picture of the things that motivate me, I have disciplined myself to focus on getting to the next level. I have learned valuable lessons along the way that have given me the confidence to move on to a higher level, while still being aware of the importance of the lower levels.

As you are introduced to each level know that it is essential to master them in the order in which they are presented. You can't jump around or skip to a higher level without fully completing each preceding level. It should always become a goal to strive to succeed at a level higher than where you are now.

LIVING LEVEL 1: BASIC NEEDS

This pertains to the most basic survival needs, such as having food, shelter, water, and daily nutrition. Before purchasing that awesome 42-inch Blu-ray flat screen television set, you must first establish yourself with the fundamentals of living. Your home or apartment should be affordable and you should have enough money in your budget to pay the utilities on time each month.

My parents instilled in me early in my adult life the importance of living within your means. They posted a list on the refrigerator of all their monthly expenses and when they were due. The expenses were always paid first, and if there was anything left over, my parents would spring for a treat. I remember as a young kid we visited my grandparents every Sunday night. On the way home we passed a Dunkin

Donuts shop. I could smell the freshness of the donuts even from the back seat of our car. I remember never saying a word about stopping, but I would certainly hope for the best. Once in a great while—I'd say about 10% of the time—Dad stopped for a treat. It was awesome! I will never forget the look on my brother and sisters' faces: We earned a treat!

Sure, we probably were angels that evening and deserved a donut, but in all honesty I think it had more to do with the fact that my parents wanted to instill in us the fact that you can't always have what you crave until you know all of the basic necessities you have provided for. It was more important to make sure the utilities in the house were paid, and that there was gas in the car and shoes on our feet. Once those were taken care of, it was okay to enjoy a treat every once in a while.

When Marilyn and I were first married we lived in a small upstairs apartment in the suburbs of Buffalo. We were barely earning more than minimum wage. She worked at Tops supermarket, and I was a merchandiser for Coca-Cola. We drove an old Ford Pinto with bald tires. We often got stuck in the snow! But we were not unhappy. We learned to live within our means and we created budgets for paying the rent, paying back my student loans, and buying groceries. We bought furniture from yard sales and planned the amount of the gas we would need to put into the car to get to work and back.

Developing good habits and prioritizing the important things in life is what it takes to master this first level. I know it's no frills; that's why it's called basic. Sure, we were tempted to go out and buy nice clothes and nicer furniture, but we knew we had to put these simple fundamentals in place. We could have gotten caught up in credit card debt and poor credit ratings (which we really didn't understand at the time), which have a tendency to spiral in the wrong direction. So, we learned to pay our bills on time, maintain a nice home, and live within our means.

Today, many years later, I see my own children enjoying a comfortable lifestyle. We often try to tell them how we first started off, but they weren't there to experience it. I think one of the most important lessons I teach them will be the importance of setting a budget and tracking their expenses. It took us twenty-three years to earn our current lifestyle. I don't want them to join us right away. They need to earn it their own way.

We all must learn to build our wealth:

- Learn to "act your wage." In my opinion, your money is 80 percent behavior and 20 percent knowledge. You have to avoid debt. Spend based on your income.
- Seven out of ten American households have too much month left for their money. Don't be a part of the majority here.
- Learn to say "NO" to frivolous spending.
- Develop a monthly budget for your money—for gas, food, utilities, clothing, and entertainment.

I learned to track my expenses at an early age. I was always frugal. When I was 13 years old I was a paperboy for the *Buffalo Courier-Express*, a morning newspaper.

Despite the snow and terribly cold winters (that seemed to last for eight months), I began a savings account. I saved $592 by collecting dimes and quarters on the route. I was careful with my spending, as my parents instilled in me the value of saving for college and to always have an emergency fund. I still have that money today! It is now my duty to share my experiences and habits with my kids.

It's not easy to pay off your bills and save money. But it's not hard either. With proper discipline and planning you can do it too. I have found that keeping a log of expenses allows me to understand my spending patterns year after year. I use both Quicken and Quickbooks computer programs. They even allow me to track my accounts online and I can log in the actual expenses by category (for year-end tax purposes). The more you understand your finances, the more you'll be able to do something about them. It's just common sense.

LIVING THE DREAM

Learn about money from old rich guys. Ben Franklin once said: "There's nothing as uncommon as common sense."

It's critical to master Level 1. It's the foundation for all future levels. Don't worry about the past. You can only control the present. Begin now to focus clearly on your goals and aspirations. Once you conquer this first level you can then advance to the next level.

LIVING LEVEL 2: SAFETY AND SECURITY

The focus here is on staying out of harm's way. The need to feel safe—living in the right neighborhood, away from crime, drug traffic, and potential injury—is essential to your well being. Developing and maintaining relationships with family, friends, neighbors, and co-workers will give you refuge.

After Marilyn and I were married for a year or so and felt good about our jobs (even though we weren't earning much) we were confident enough about our finances to begin looking to purchase our own home. We consulted with a real estate agent and together determined we could afford a home, but nothing expensive or lavish. What was important to us was to find a house in a nice neighborhood. We wanted to feel comfortable and safe, as we knew we would soon begin having children. We found a home in Tonawanda, New York, just one block from the Niagara River where we could walk the dog (and eventually push a baby stroller). We paid $42,000 for this ranch home in 1988. It was the perfect starter house with three bedrooms, a full basement, and a nice yard. This is where we began our family, and we still rave about that little house today.

We lived in this house for four years, paying our bills

regularly and on time. I took a job with a car rental company and then jumped into the insurance industry as a sales agent. I took classes on leadership and public speaking. I placed a strong focus on developing relationships with my friends and co-workers. I sought advice from others who were already doing the things I wanted to do. Marilyn and I also realized the importance of staying close with our family—our parents, brothers, and sisters. We would need help and support (and babysitters!) if we wanted to continue our quest for lifelong happiness and living our dreams. We were very fortunate our family was so supportive of us.

My career was beginning to take off. I had begun earning a good living and our savings and investments were growing. Then, and only then, did we decide to upgrade to a larger home.

The key to mastering Level 2 is to take your time. Don't jump into something before you are ready, just so you can get started on the next level. That's not how it works. Living a successful life requires time and patience. Stay within your means and plan accordingly. Be sure to take calculated risks.

LIVING LEVEL 3: I BELONG

You and I need to feel that we're a part of a community—a caring group. This could be a church group, a neighborhood of caring people, or a bonding with co-workers.

We all need to feel appreciated. We feel good knowing we are a part of a bigger picture where we optimize our strengths and use them for something good.

Joining civic clubs, a church, or charity groups goes a long way in achieving this level of satisfaction. Personal growth comes when we learn the importance of helping others. I realize most people don't volunteer in their community or help those less fortunate to win an award or to receive special recognition, but helping others does make you feel needed. And when we are needed, we are appreciated.

While we were still living in our first home in Tonawanda, I joined the volunteer fire department, the Union Hook and Ladder #1. One of my lifelong goals was to be a fireman, and now I had my chance. I took the mandatory "Essentials" training course and soon became a full-fledged fireman. I remember having a scanner at the side of my bed, and my entire fire gear in the trunk of my car, a 1978 Plymouth Horizon. (I bought that car as a result of a golf game with my friend Mark Hazuda after our Pinto died. We bet $10 a hole to see how much I would have to pay. It cost $130 as a result of my poor putting).

Several times a week I would get the call for a house fire or car accident. One time I had to battle a blaze of used tires piled a mountain high, the fire lasted the entire night. Another time I remember being one of only a few firefighters at a burning house at eight in the morning. Most of the other volunteer firefighters were unavailable because they were already off to their day jobs. I was still at home that morning because I didn't have a sales appointment until later in the day. The house was fully engulfed when the other volunteers and I arrived on the scene. We worked well together to assess the situation and focus on our priorities. We had to get the mother and children out of the house. They left wearing the clothes on their backs—their pajamas and with nothing else. We battled the fire with all our might, but unfortunately it was a total loss. The family was unharmed, but they lost everything.

A couple of things entered my mind during this time in my life. One, I was in the insurance business, and it was my duty to help people properly insure their home and cars. I had witnessed firsthand how devastation can strike a family. I didn't need to be a pushy salesperson; instead, I simply had to do my job and tell a story like this, and the importance of having insurance becomes clear.

The second thing I began to feel was the importance of belonging. I was a fireman. I was in a position to help others. I was a part of something. The guys at the department were my friends. We shared something in common. Oftentimes after a fire call we would meet back at the station, have a beer or two, and discuss the recent fire call—what went right and what went wrong. We also held functions with our families, such as picnics and dances. The fire hall was one of the first places we ever took our son Mikey after he was born in 1990. Marilyn was comfortable with the other wives and families. We proudly marched in all the community parades and planned chicken BBQ's and fundraisers. We were getting out of the house, building relationships with people beyond just work associates and family.

TODAY'S NETWORKING

It's interesting to witness the phenomenal growth of social media (Facebook, Twitter, etc.) in our world today. I believe it is a direct result of people wanting to belong to something. Just as I developed the need to associate with my fellow firefighters, I see people connecting today in ways never before dreamed of, regardless of their location. I must admit I enjoy entering my own posts on social media sites because I know my "friends" will see it and know what I'm doing. I seek their connection, approval, and instant feedback and it makes me feel good. In all honesty, most of the entries are mundane-sounding, even to me, but it lets people respond to me immediately and without much effort. In the old days (it really wasn't that long ago) we had to write letters or send e-mails to get a response. Now we get it immediately. Text messaging works in the same way, too—immediate feedback without having to wait more than a minute or two.

Facebook and Twitter have revolutionized the way we communicate with each other. The bottom line is that we need to do something and have relationships that will allow us to fit in. Having a lot of friends on the computer allows us to feel good about ourselves. I would challenge you to use your ability beyond simple social networking and get involved in causes that will make a difference in the lives of others. Volunteer at your local hospital, join a church group or a local Rotary club, and engage with both the cause and the people you will meet.

We all have something valuable to offer. And there are

many people out there who need us. Your challenge will be to join communities where you can make a positive impact. Instead of spending several hours a day on your computer, my advice to you is to be involved in causes that will bring positive and long-lasting results. The rewards you will feel will be those of gratitude, understanding, and appreciation. When you've accomplished this you will have mastered Level 3.

LIVING THE DREAM

When we are needed by others we feel appreciated and that's a good feeling!

LIVING LEVEL 4: HIGH REGARD AND SELF-RESPECT

Being in high regard comes from feeling liked by others for your personal traits, habits, and qualities. You feel respected by others. Your skills and knowledge about your areas of expertise are being used for the common good. Here, you find yourself taking leadership roles in your work, your family, and your community.

As a young fireman I took time to observe and learn from my superiors. In the years thereafter I joined various church groups as well as the United Way organization. I enjoyed going to the board meetings and keeping up with their pressing issues—mainly fundraising and planning upcoming community events. But I rarely spoke up and gave my opinion. As time passed I began to realize that I knew more about these organizations and their particular needs than I thought I did. It was my turn to step up and speak up.

By getting involved and sharing your strengths you become confident in your ability to make a difference. It may begin with small things, but over time you will develop into a person who is sought after for advice and counsel. You will create stronger and more satisfying friendships that will be extremely rewarding. You will be helping others in a manner that is desperately needed, and our world will be a better place thanks to your efforts.

Now, I am heavily involved as chairperson of the board of my local United Way, and I serve on many community boards. I don't perform these activities to impress people; rather, I perform them in an effort to share my talents with others in a productive manner.

If you don't think you have time to volunteer, start small. Get involved in something you feel strongly about. Then, as you become more comfortable you can begin to express your ideas and feelings in an attempt to improve the situation.

LIVING THE DREAM

You earn self-respect when you commit to a higher power. Trust and pray your strengths will be used in productive ways.

LIVING LEVEL 5: SELF ACTUALIZATION

This is the highest level of all. It involves the desire to truly understand what your place in life is all about. It is about reaching your full potential. It is about a feeling you get when you know you've done the right thing and will continue to press on.

Growth doesn't end. It continues. Constant and never-ending improvement in all areas of your life is achieved and it's done gracefully. That's what self actualization is—and, on some level, you already know it!

Maslow identified positive qualities:

- The need to be creative rather than stagnant. Having a sense of uncertainty in your life is a good thing. It propels growth.
- The need to enjoy fresh experiences and avoid boredom. Go back to the **Life Balance** survey in Chapter One to see where you are at this current moment in your life. Where can you improve?
- The need to use your talents and abilities and not waste them.

- The need to be stretched and challenged in your skills. Remember to *"do something every day that scares you!"*
- The need to feel that you are helping to make this world a better place.
- The need to experience aesthetic pleasure and delight.

Each and every day the challenge will be to satisfy all these needs and experience growth. It doesn't end at the top of this one mountain. There are many mountains still out there. They need to be scaled and mastered.

There is no time for rest; the world is moving too fast. Take note of your accomplishments and use the experiences when future opportunities are presented to you.

You will come to know the areas of your life that need focus and other areas that you may be able to eliminate. The "joy of quitting" is something that should be taken very seriously. As you get involved in many activities there may come a time where you need to eliminate some things. If the time feels right to step aside, or you feel your work is complete in a particular field so you can perhaps free up some time for another project, it's okay to say "no."

LIVING THE DREAM

*The greatest sense of fulfillment comes from knowing **why** you exist and then doing something about it. You were put on this earth for a reason. It's up to you to find out what that reason is.*

PILLAR 2
In Pursuit of Giving

TEN REASONS TO READ TO YOUR CHILDREN

1. Because when you hold them and give them this attention, they know you love them.
2. Because reading to them will encourage them to become readers.
3. Because children's books today are so good that they are fun, even for adults.
4. Children's book illustrations often rank with the best, giving them a lifelong feeling for good art.
5. Books are one way of passing on your moral values. Readers know how to put themselves in other's shoes.
6. Because every teacher and librarian they ever encounter will thank you.
7. Because, until they learn how to read themselves, they will think you are magic.
8. Because it's nostalgic.
9. Because, for that short space of time, they will stay clean and,
10. Because, if you do, they may then let you read in peace.

—AUTHOR UNKNOWN

Chapter 7

IT'S YOUR DUTY TO SERVE

"You cannot live a perfect day without doing something for someone who will never be able to repay you."

JOHN WOODEN
UCLA BASKETBALL COACH WHO WON 10 NCAA CHAMPIONSHIPS

Back when my son Peter, Jr., was just 4 years old he was playing with his older brother and injured his leg. After a quick trip to the local hospital, it was determined that he had a fracture above his knee, and he would have to be transferred to Buffalo Children's Hospital, where they had a specialized unit. Here he spent the next three weeks of his young life, laid up in traction while his knee and thigh were stretched so they would begin to grow back in place properly.

Marilyn never left his bedside while I made several trips back to our home three hours away, while also finding babysitters for our other two children.

Because I was so worried about missing time at work myself, I had the clever idea of bringing my laptop computer into the hospital room with me and set up my own work station so I could keep working. Back then it wasn't as easy to get Internet access, but somehow I rigged enough wires to make it work. Heaven only knows if I mixed up the wires on my computer with any of the important wires the hospital may have needed for their uses; however, everything seemed to work out fine.

I was proud of myself as I worked away in the room, while Marilyn tended to Peter, Jr.'s needs. He was a hurting young boy, restless and frustrated that he couldn't move in his bed. I kept working. After a few days I began to notice how many people were entering the room to check up on us. Sure, the doctors and nurses kept a close eye on Peter's progress, and his meals were delivered at the same time every day. But what I also saw was a parade of volunteers who would come in to the room to say hello to us, and even spend some time playing games with our son. They played video games, colored in the coloring books, and even marveled as he showed them all of his Power Ranger action figures.

It struck me funny that these complete strangers were showing such concern for us. And they just weren't simple, obligatory visits. They were thoughtful and genuine. I began to wonder why these people were doing this. They weren't getting paid for this work, and they were spending time away from their own family and friends to come to a hospital ward full of complete strangers, most whom they'd never see again after they left.

MY TRANSFORMATION

This was a magical moment for me, personally. There I was, the father of this young boy, sitting in the corner of this hospital room doing my work, while complete strangers were tending to my child. They had this boy smiling, giggling, and talking, while I was off in my own world worrying about sales quotas and performance reviews.

I remember driving home by myself later that night with tears in my eyes. I was not doing all the things I was capable of doing. Although I was physically in the room, I was not mentally "there." I was not tending to my own family, and I felt terrible for this. I also began thinking about my entire life. What was missing? Was I doing everything I was capable of doing to be fulfilled?

I knew I had talents to offer. I knew I had treasures to offer. I began thinking of how I could begin to use my God-given abilities to help others.

It was at that point in my life that I decided to get involved in community service work and giving to others. I placed a call to my church and spoke to a lady named Rosemary Bloise. I asked her what I could do to get involved. She immediately suggested I use my public speaking skills and volunteer to be a religious education teacher, right there at our church. She needed help with the eighth-grade class. As wild as it sounded, I agreed. And from that point on, I committed my life to helping others.

Giving back makes you a more complete person. It took me over thirty years to realize that. But now I know its importance. It makes others feel good, and it makes ME feel good about myself.

By the way, Peter, Jr., made a complete recovery after spending a long time in rehabilitation. In some ways I, too, completed a rehabilitation of my own life. And I'm grateful for the opportunity now to give, advocate and volunteer.

COMMUNITY INVOLVEMENT

In the LIFE PLANNING FOR A BALANCED YOU survey in Chapter 1 there is a series of questions centered around community involvement. I know you understand that you don't volunteer for your own fame or recognition. Rather, you do it because it's good for your soul.

I've heard people say they give to charity each year when they toss a few coins into the kettle next to the Salvation Army worker who is ringing a bell outside the retail store during the Christmas holiday season. While this is fine, there needs to be more. Without me preaching here, I want to emphasize that giving to your church or your favorite charity should include more than just giving your money. When you volunteer your time and your talents to these causes, you will be helping both the organization AND yourself.

FIND A WAY TO SERVE

"It's one of those beautiful compensations of this life that no man can sincerely try to help another without helping himself."

RALPH WALDO EMERSON
(1803-1882) AMERICAN PHILOSOPHER AND POET

The greatest level of self-satisfaction is experienced when you and I find a way to serve others. There are many opportunities where you can use your business skills (management, accounting, fundraising, volunteer recruitment) or your personal skills (high energy, enthusiasm, care, and concern for others).

If you have a talent (we all have something to offer), consider working on charitable events. You can work at the visible community events (church bazaars, etc.) or behind the scenes serving on the board of a nonprofit organization.

LIVING THE DREAM

Get involved and learn how you can help others in your community. This is a major step in your quest for improved Life Balance and ultimate happiness.

Chapter 8

VOLUNTEER, AND VOLUNTEER OFTEN

"I slept, and I dreamt that life was all joy. I woke, and saw all that life was but service. I served, and discovered that service was joy."

R. TAGORE
(1861-1941) POET, NOVELIST, MUSICIAN AND PHILOSOPHER

To be a *volunteer* is to put into the practice of working on behalf of others without being motivated by financial or material gain. To me, volunteering is generally considered an altruistic activity, intended to promote good or improve human quality of life. People also volunteer to gain skills without requiring an employer's financial investment.

Volunteering takes many forms and is performed by a wide range of people. Many volunteers are specifically trained in the areas they work in, such as medicine, education, or emergency rescue. Others volunteer on an as-needed basis, such as in response to a natural disaster. If you're like me, you are a busy person—work, household duties, family responsibility—but there are people and organizations out there that need you.

BENEFITS OF VOLUNTEERING

There are two major benefits that come from activities of service to the community:

1. **Economic benefits:** These are activities undertaken by volunteers that would otherwise have to be funded by the state or by private capital, so volunteering adds to the overall economic output of a country and reduces the burden on government spending. Instead of seeing your taxes raised, volunteer labor can be used to complete a task that otherwise would have to be funded and worked by paid labor.

2. **Social benefits:** Volunteering helps to build more cohesive communities, fostering greater trust between citizens and developing norms of solidarity and reciprocity that are essential to stable communities.

DO YOU HAVE ONE HOUR A WEEK THAT YOU CAN SPARE? That's all it takes. Think about your talents:

- Are you good with a hammer? Can you build or repair things? **Habitat for Humanity** may need a handy person like you.

- Do you like to drive around your community and visit people who may have a need for basic items like a home-cooked meal? **Meals on Wheels** may need a caring person like you.

- Do you like to plan events that bring members of the community together to fight a specific cause? The **American Cancer Society Relay for Life** or **Susan B. Komen** annual "Race for the Cure" may need a talented person like you.

- Do you like to contact or visit area businesses to solicit funds to help strengthen the local community? Your **United Way Organization** may be the answer.

- Do you like to work with other people just like you on projects like improving literacy in your local elementary schools or wiping out polio in the world? Perhaps your local **Rotary** or **Kiwanis** club would be of interest to you.

This is just a sample of what's available to you right in your own community. And most of these organizations require just a little bit of your time. I speak from experience that being a volunteer is not only beneficial to the people or organizations in need, but rewarding to YOU as well.

LIVING THE DREAM

After the game, the king and the pawn go in the same box.

NO MORE PROCRASTINATION—NO MORE WAITING

We have all been put on this earth for a reason. Many people spend their entire life trying to figure out what that reason is. They sit around day after day, year after year, waiting for something to happen or waiting to be told what to do.

I like the way Dr. Seuss
(Oh, The Places You'll Go) puts it:

Many people spend their life waiting
Waiting for a train to go
Or a bus to come, or a plane to go,
Or the mail to come, or the rain to go
Or the phone to ring, or the snow to snow
Or waiting around for a Yes or No
Or waiting for their hair to grow
Everyone is just waiting…
NO!
That's not for you!

Somehow you'll escape
All that waiting and staying
You'll find the bright places
Where boom bands are playing

Oh, the places you'll go! There is fun to be done!
There are points to be scored. There are games to

be won...
And you will succeed
Yes, you will, indeed.

IT'S TIME TO TAKE ACTION!

So, get involved. Get engaged. And do it now! Start with just one hour per week. If you like it, it won't seem like work. Trust me. Begin to put activities into your schedule that you know you can complete. No excuses about finding time. Perhaps you have to cut back a bit on watching television or that extra hour of sleep. It's worth it!

"The world is entering a new time zone, and one of the most difficult adjustments people must make is in their fundamental concepts and beliefs about the management of time."

DAN SULLIVAN
PRESIDENT, THE STRATEGIC COACH

BE PASSIONATE ABOUT YOUR COMMITMENT

You know yourself and your abilities. All you need to do is get engaged in an activity that you have a strong belief in. If you don't know, then begin doing some research. Read the local newspaper to see what event is coming up that might spark your interest. Instead of just attending, maybe you can work at the event. Ask your family and friends what charities they are involved with, and if there's room for you. Spend time checking out websites of local associations and you might be surprised what you find. Some may be very in depth and appealing. If you find yourself inspired to find out more information, you may have found your passion.

EDUCATE YOURSELF

Make an investment and learn as much as possible about the cause in which you have an interest. Find books and browse Internet sites to become fully aware of the history and the primary reasons they exist. You can learn about the financial needs and how they are funded. You can learn about the management structure. You can learn about the impact the organization has on the local community and perhaps a broader area.

The more you know about the organization, the more you can determine your area of interest. Even the smallest of details can help.

LEARN FROM THE EXPERTS

A few years ago my sister Linda and I signed up to go to an Anthony Robbins Seminar in New York City. There were several well-known speakers who were going to be at the event, including Donald Trump, Barbara Walters, Christopher Reeve, and Larry King. When we told our mother about it, she jumped up and said she wanted to go, too.

The three of us stayed at a hotel in New Jersey. We stayed up half the night talking about our lives and wondering why we had decided to make this trip together and what it would do for us. We weren't sure what God had planned for us; we just knew our fate and destiny were to be molded at this seminar.

The seminar itself was a fast-paced event filled with loud music and fanfare. Over 10,000 people were there. Most of the speakers talked about their accomplishments and the fact that they were committed in some way to helping others. Barbara Walters talked about her early career and dealing with the fact that she was a female reporter in a male-dominated industry.

Donald Trump talked about overcoming the ups and downs of the real estate investment market and how he always seemed to find a way to end up on top. Despite circumstances around him that he could not always control, he learned to take calculated risks. And while others backed down from big investment deals in troubling financial times, he jumped in with two feet and never looked back.

Christopher Reeve then came out onto the stage. He was the former *Superman* movie star who suffered a paralyzing injury while riding a horse. We had tears in our eyes as we watched him being wheeled on stage. He needed help from a respirator attached to his throat just to talk. As he began to speak the audience was silent, listening to only his sounds. He explained that he was grateful to be alive and that he now understood his purpose for life. He was committed to helping other paralyzed people cope with their situation while spearheading fundraising and awareness efforts aimed at finding a cure for spinal cord injuries.

LEAVE IT TO MOM

My mother was excited! As the day wore on, instead of getting tired, she got focused. She had found another calling. Even though she successfully raised five wonderful children and now had a truckload of grandchildren, she had a desire to do more. She was looking to find a way to help others in her community who needed basic clothing and food.

Within days of returning home, Mom contacted her church and immediately began work with the Outreach Center at St. Christopher's Church. She and the other volunteers opened a facility in the basement of the church where needy families could come to get clothing, boots, and winter coats. And in Buffalo, they certainly were needed!

A few times during the year, special collections were taken and these items are boxed up and sent to countries in places such as Africa and in South America, where they would be put to good use.

You're never too old to educate yourself. You're never too old to go to a seminar, take a class, or read a new book. And you're never too old to get involved. Take a lesson from my mother. In her 80s, bad knees and all, she still works every week at the Outreach Center making life better for those less fortunate than her. In the end, she is still growing!

The **economic benefits** of volunteer work can often be measured in financial terms. The **social benefits** are measured in terms of pride, satisfaction, making good friends, and serving others.

LIVING THE DREAM

Create a community around yourself with committed people just like you—to help you with your cause. You will get a sense of fulfillment that will make you want to do even more.

Chapter 9

THE LAW OF RECIPROCITY

"You better get to livin', givin', don't forget to throw in a little forgivin' and love along the way."

DOLLY PARTON
AMERICAN SINGER-SONGWRITER, ACTRESS AND PHILANTHROPIST

The **law of reciprocity**, also known as the **Golden Rule,** is an ethical code that states one has a right to just treatment, and a responsibility to ensure justice for others. Reciprocity is arguably the most essential basis for the modern concept of human rights.

A key element of the Golden Rule is that a person attempting to live by this rule treats all people, not just members of his or her in-group, with consideration. When consideration is given it usually is returned to you, often at greater levels.

DO UNTO OTHERS

I was in church recently zipping up my coat as the final song began from the choir. There was an elderly lady standing alone just a few feet away from me. She had been singing throughout the service and I noticed how pretty her voice was. It wasn't incredible, but it was very pleasant. I could tell she enjoyed using her vocal chords. I wondered to myself, *Should I give her a compliment?* I didn't want to embarrass myself, or her for that matter, but I felt the urge to say something.

As the song began to wind down I leaned toward her, tapped her on the shoulder (she was still singing), and whispered to her, "I just want to tell you that you have a beautiful voice."

She paused for a moment and then I could see a large smile on her face grow right in front of me. She then replied, "Oh, thank you. You have truly made my day!"

I'll bet that person went out of church walking on air. Someone had noticed her and took the time to pay her a compliment. Odds are she went home and told her family about it. She probably hummed a nice tune to herself the rest of the day.

What was I trying to do? Was I trying to get something out of this encounter?

The answer is nothing. All I wanted to do was pass on a bit of honest appreciation and bring a little happiness to someone without expecting something in return.

HOW TO WIN FRIENDS

One of my favorite books of all time is Dale Carnegie's *How to Win Friends and Influence People* (Simon and Schuster, 1936). It has sold over 20 million copies worldwide. The book describes remarkably simple methods for how to get people to like you:

- Become genuinely interested in others. By being real and sincere they will show their appreciation toward you and call you a friend.

- A person's name is to that person the sweetest and most important sound in any language. People love to hear their name. Take the time to get to know a person's name and use it often in your conversation.

- Be a good listener, and encourage other people to talk about themselves. Ask questions and be attentive as you hear their responses.

- Talk in terms of other people's interests. Find out their interests, hobbies, favorite sports teams, etc. It will allow you to bring up these topics in future conversations and will show them that you were paying attention.

- Make the other person feel important, and do it sincerely.

While writing my first book, *In Pursuit of Business,* I dedicated an entire chapter to learning ways to meet people and become genuinely interested in them. I outlined a series of Dale Carnegie memorization clues that has become part of the world-famous class in Effective Communications and Human Relations®. Here, you learn and utilize a set of questions to ask people to get to know them better. It works great when you first meet someone and you're trying to get past the awkward moments of silence. I actually had to seek permission from the Dale Carnegie and Associates, Inc. headquarters in New York City to share this concept. After my relentless pursuit they agreed (as long as I gave them credit in my book) and the chapter was born. I was told that this was the first time they had ever granted permission for this method to be used by someone without actually enrolling in a Dale Carnegie class.

Getting to know people and ultimately getting them to like you is critical in all areas of life: personal, work, and community. You can never have too many friends. And when you develop the skills to get to know people better, they will flock toward you. And they will like you back!

Always make the other person feel important. Carnegie says the "desire to be important is the deepest urge in human nature." It's the craving to feel appreciated, needed, and wanted. All it takes is the ability to carry a conversation with them and show how interested you are.

When I talk to prospective clients about their insurance needs I find myself asking a lot of questions. The more questions I ask, the more people will open up and talk to me. I once spent an entire hour talking to someone and I never made a comment of my own; I just asked questions.

The person went on and on and shared more about himself than I would otherwise have ever known. At the end of the hour the person I was taking to commented what a nice person I was. Well, sure I was, but the entire conversation was about him.

Philosophers throughout history—Confucius, Lao-Tse, Buddha—have preached the rules of relationships as the most critical rule of happiness. Jesus taught it over two thousand years ago, and it's probably the most important rule in the world: "Do unto others as you would have done unto you."

We all want the approval of those we meet. We want to feel important and we want to feel loved. And so, we obey the Golden Rule and give unto others what we would have others give to us.

Giving to others brings out the best in all of us. Good intentions bring good rewards. Gestures of kindness without expecting something in return makes you feel inner peace. It doesn't have to be a big deal; it can be simple gesture like holding the door for someone or waving ahead the person who arrived at in intersection the same time as you. The more you practice, the better you will become.

LIVING THE DREAM

How? When? And Where should you use the Golden Rule? The answer is ALL THE TIME.

PILLAR 3

In Pursuit of Sharing

"The greatest education in the world is watching the masters at work."

MICHAEL JACKSON
(1958-2009) THE "KING OF POP," AMERICAN MUSICIAN AND ENTERTAINER

Chapter 10

BE A COMMUNICATOR

"I hear and I forget. I see and I remember. I do and I understand."

CHINESE PROVERB

Our world will never forget September 11, 2001, when we were rocked with disaster and fear. Our safe and somewhat comfortable world was now wounded. If you were old enough to remember, I'm sure the day is vivid in your mind.

A few weeks earlier, I had been asked to give a homily at our Catholic church on a small group faith formation program we were about to embark upon. It was called RENEW. Although this was rarely done, our priest wanted me, as a simple churchgoer, to deliver the fifteen-minute talk from the pulpit at all three weekend services. The scheduled date was September 23rd.

How was I supposed to deliver a speech less than two weeks after this tragedy that has changed America forever? I remember calling the priest, and he asked me to continue with the speech, despite what had happened in our world. I said, "Are you sure, Father?" somewhat hoping he would ask to postpone my talk. He urged me to proceed and do my best.

Whatever I had planned to talk about to the 1500 parishioners had changed. I thought about what I would say, and I prayed I would have the courage and the ability to say it well. When Sunday came, I went to the podium and the entire church was silent. Many of the people knew me, but obviously had no idea what I was going to talk about. But here was my chance—my chance to communicate with them.

I began by saying:
"We should all be thankful for the beautiful things we have in our lives—especially our family and loved ones, and our friends and neighbors that had come forth to pray and hold each other in this most challenging of times. I know that somehow this terrible tragedy is a reminder that we should all be very careful not to take anything for granted. Life is so very precious. And it is not guaranteed. Through the support of our community and of all the communities across America something is happening that was setting a marvelous tone."

I then quoted our then-president, George W. Bush:
"We are now at war—a war between freedom and love. Live your lives, hug your children, be calm and resolute. Pull the values of America in a fight for our principles These have always been our strengths—we need to make it our mission now."

I paused for a moment and looked at the congregation, who was attached to these words.

I then continued:
"We are all reacting to these recent events, but we need to do more. It is our long-term response that will matter most. A response is our well-thought-out plan to change our lives in a positive way. We need to model and experience ***community, patriotism, faith, love, and hope.*** *We need to support one another, pray together, and share our faith openly."*

I could see the reaction of the congregation. They were nodding their heads in support. I then said the words I will always regard as a telling statement for that moment and many moments since:

"I can't help but think that God is now so very proud of you, God is now so very proud of me..... God is now so very proud of all of us."

TAKE ACTION

I finished the talk by inviting anyone who was interested to join a small group that would gather in the warmth of someone's living room and talk about life, values, hope, and relationships with God. We had over 200 people sign up, which allowed us to create 20 groups of 10 people each. Some of these groups still exist and meet today, almost a decade later.

Communication is the key. Take a chance and tell people what you think. Tell them what you'd like them to do. Tell them how much support you can give them. Encourage them. And tell them what they will learn.

Savor the opportunity to get up in front of a crowd and share your insights. You don't need to brag or dictate every action you'd like them to take. Instead, feed them with thoughts and ideas that will lead to achieving a higher level of growth, satisfaction, and internal rewards.

A good communicator will ultimately become a good leader. By speaking to individuals and groups about the causes you believe in you will develop a confidence far beyond measurement. Our world needs leaders to step up and share their skills. Challenge yourself to become a better communicator; take classes like Dale Carnegie or Toastmasters. As you develop and grow into a confident speaker you will become a better person. You will be able to share your thoughts and beliefs in a better manner and will earn the trust and respect from others.

LIVING THE DREAM

Your words can be a powerful tool. Use them wisely and appropriately. Take advantage of an opportunity to share your God-given talents.

Chapter 11

BE A MENTOR

"I have learned that people will forget what you said, people will forget what you did, but people will never forget how you made them feel."

ALBERT SCHWEITZER
(1875-1965) GERMAN-FRENCH THEOLOGIAN, MUSICIAN, PHILOSOPHER AND PHYSICIAN

Every so often someone enters your life and leaves an impression on you that lasts forever. For me, I've been fortunate to have several examples where these fine people not only become my friends but also my mentors. A mentor is a trusted friend, counselor, or teacher, usually a more experienced person. Some professions have "mentoring programs" in which newcomers are paired with more experienced people, who advise them and serve as examples as they advance. Schools sometimes offer mentoring programs to new students, or students having difficulties.

I've always felt young. When I graduated from high

school I was only 17 years old. After four years of college at Binghamton University I was just 21. I met Marilyn and was married shortly after my 24th birthday. I got a job at Coca-Cola for a few years and then worked at a car rental agency near the Buffalo International Airport. I was promoted to general manager at the age of 25.

I soon switched careers and entered the insurance industry. I was quickly promoted into management at the ripe age of 27. I had such baby face I usually had to show proof of age just to enter a bar. I was energetic and full of ideas.

As a district sales manager for Nationwide Insurance I found myself working with people twice my age. My fellow managers were all in their 40s and 50s, and my sales force was about the same. As a young "kid," I often sat back and took in their knowledge and experience. I learned to show respect for who they were and what they knew. And, I learned what I did not know!

Most of my peers were much older than I was, but they treated me with dignity. They knew I was educated and had a desire to learn more. I found myself spending time with as many of them as I could. One in particular was Gerry Shallcross.

Gerry was a fellow district sales manager for Nationwide Insurance in a territory adjacent to mine. (I was in Buffalo; he was in Rochester.) We got together quite regularly to share ideas on selling, recruiting, and training our sales agents. He taught me the value of treating each person as if he or she is the most important person in the world. Sure, you had to challenge people and share your expectations with them, but you didn't need to force your opinions on them like a dictator.

> **LIVING THE DREAM**
>
> *People do not want to be treated equally. Rather, they want to be treated individually.*

Gerry shared with me that I shouldn't be concerned about reaching a quota or winning a company trip to an exotic tropical resort. Rather, I should focus on helping my agents become better marketers, salespeople and experts in customer service. The results would come naturally if the job was performed properly and with dignity.

I learned that I should not deal with every person I met the same way. Each had unique circumstances that needed unique attention. So, I began by developing relationships with my sales agents. (I was in charge of over 25 of them.) I asked questions and I soaked up as much knowledge as I could. I observed their operations and took as many notes as I could. I then asked Gerry his advice as I prepared my plan to help these agents grow profitable businesses for themselves.

As my career continued I placed a lot of my field experience into my "knowledge bank." I never knew when I would need it, but when the situation arose, I felt prepared to deal with it. Gerry was with me along the way; he was my biggest cheerleader. For the 11 years that followed I recruited, trained, and developed many new sales agents. I gleaned the knowledge I learned from one agent and shared it with others, just like Gerry had taught me. Today, many of these agents are living very successful lives, and I feel good about that.

REMEMBER THE MENTORS IN YOUR UPBRINGING

Another mentor of mine was the regional sales manager for Nationwide Insurance, Merv Bartholow. He was my boss for several years as I began to grow into an effective manager. The two of us decided to take a Dale Carnegie public speaking course together. Once a week for 12 weeks we went to a night class and gave two- or three-minute speeches on various topics. It was a great way to overcome the fear of talking in front of a group. The morning after each class, Merv and I would sip coffee in his office and discuss ways in which we both could improve our speaking skills. He was already a good speaker, but I think he was putting himself in this situation just to build MY confidence. I took away valuable advice from him on posture, animation, and how to use humor in my talks. Although he was a busy man he took the time to nurture our relationship and help me better understand the need to be a good communicator in front of a group. I now teach classes about public speaking, and I owe a large part of my success to Merv.

I've been extremely fortunate over the years to have a whole series of friends who I consider to be my mentors. These men and women taught me about leadership, relationship building, and running my own business. When one mentor moved on another mentor arrived, willing to share his or her life experiences. I've learned from the people in my Rotary club, the church organizations, and business networking groups I've belonged to, and even in day-to-day dealings with my insurance clients. Many have shared with me the value of accomplishing the important things in life as well as giving me the understanding that I must always give back my personal time, talents, and treasures to others who are in need.

LIVING THE DREAM

When the student is ready
the teacher will appear.

NOW IT'S YOUR TURN

"Study anyone who's great, and you'll find that they apprenticed to a master, or several masters. Therefore, if you want to achieve greatness, renown and superlative success, you must apprentice to a master."

ROBERT ALLEN,
CO-AUTHOR OF *THE ONE MINUTE MILLIONAIRE*
(HARMONY BOOKS, 2002)

You have your own talents and treasures that have made you into the person you now are. By now I'm sure you realize the importance of giving back. It's one of the most valuable lessons you'll take from reading this book. It's now time for you to go forward and share your own experiences (good and bad) with others. There's a whole new crop of people out there who are starving for knowledge about:

- How to find a job.
- How to complete their education.
- How to develop a trade or skill.
- How to meet people and form relationships.
- How to change a flat tire.
- How to understand their finances.
- How to overcome grief and emotional stress.

You and I have something special to offer. In our own unique way we have learned valuable lessons that MUST now be shared with others.

There's no benefit to holding it inside any longer. Offer your assistance where you think it is needed and you see an opportunity: your family, co-workers, business associates, and even a complete stranger.

LIVING THE DREAM

Our rewards in life are in exact proportion to our contributions, our service to others. Learn from your mentors and then share that knowledge with others.

Chapter 12

BE YOURSELF

"The grass must bend when the wind blows across it"

CONFUCIUS

You're on the treadmill—of life. Running around each day on a mission of trying to get better in everything you do. The secret, of course, is that you have a choice. You do not need to spend your time in self-pity thinking about the failures in your past, your grief, or your shame:

- Don't impress.
- Don't start an argument.
- Don't live your life over.
- Don't rush through your day.
- Don't be someone else.

Very rarely in my life was I formally taught the rules of proper daily living. Not in grammar school, high school, or college was I exposed to a class about how to handle adversities, eliminate bad habits, make friends, or be a good soul mate. Sure, my parents were loving and supportive, but there really is no formal education on this topic that you can get from a classroom or a textbook. Life for me has been a game of ups and downs, trials and errors, with good and bad results. Has it been like this for you, too?

Over the years, I've had to learn to apply myself and try to learn about the important things that really make a difference. That's pretty much why I wrote this book. I want to share my world experiences with always trying to be myself and not conforming to others just to be popular or to get a job promotion.

LEARNING A LESSON

I had been a sales manager for several years when I got the talking to. I was about 32 years old and still had a youthful look. I had a good track record for my sales district and had actually accepted a transfer (okay, it was a promotion) to a larger territory based in Elmira, New York. Our company had arranged a very special meet-and-greet session with players from the Buffalo Bills professional football team. Hall of Fame players like Jim Kelly and Steve Tasker were there to pose for photos with us and sign autographs.

I was in my glory. I was a big Bills fan, and these were my favorite players! I mingled and danced through the small crowd (this was a private party for the insurance sales team only), laughing, joking, and giving "high fives" to my sales force. I was smart enough to know not to drink alcohol, but I did wear a Bills cap on my head and posed for several pictures (which I still have today). Along the way I noticed the big state manager, Fred, watching me. He was tracking my every move. Apparently, I was doing things he didn't like.

Later we were assembled at a sales managers meeting. In front of my peers, Fred called me to the back of the room, got within 12 inches of my face, and yelled at me for a solid two minutes. He called my behavior "*flippant.*" I had not acted appropriate in his eyes and he thought I was immature and unprofessional.

I was shocked. I didn't know what to say or what to do. I didn't even know what the word *flippant* meant (but I sure do now). I walked away with my head down and went right to my hotel room. A few of my fellow managers had witnessed my lashing and knocked on my door to offer support. They said I really had not done anything wrong, but since I was much younger perhaps there was a feeling that I was a threat to the older, more experienced manager. Perhaps my likeability, enthusiastic behavior, and good track record for reaching my quotas was causing Fred not to like me. To this day, I really don't know what it was.

Nevertheless, for the next several months I sulked. I didn't know what to do or how to act. I continued to do my job and I met my sales objectives, but the fire inside of me had fizzled. One man, one conversation, deflated me. I kept my feelings to myself and didn't talk about this episode to my sales force. I tried to stay above the level of manager-bashing. Besides, many people liked him, so I simply went to work and did my job.

I thought long and hard about what I had done, who I had become, and what kind of person THEY wanted me to be. I said to myself: "You could change your personality and become a good soldier, or you could continue to be yourself and take your chances." The more I thought about it, the more I realized that I was already on the right path to success, just by being me. I liked me. I liked who I was, and the style that I used. I liked being enthusiastic, out of the ordinary, and sometimes unpredictable. Those were the traits that had defined me. Slowly but surely I went back to my old ways. But I learned to be aware that there were going to be situations in my future where some people weren't going to agree with my style or my personality.

Fred retired a short time later and at his retirement party (I went just to make sure he didn't change his mind and un-retire) he made it a point to shake my hand and wish me well. He told me he had been hard on me because he knew I had a lot of upside potential in my career, wherever that might be. I later came to appreciate the man for what he had said to me. I learned my lesson—though it was a different one than Fred thought he was teaching me! I had become a stronger person for going through the whole experience and committing to being myself.

LIVING THE DREAM

Sometimes you learn the most in life when you experience pain. Remember it's not how you react to a certain situation – it's how you respond.

RULES FOR A HAPPIER LIFE

I have spent over two decades of my life reading self-help books from authors like Napoleon Hill and Og Mandino. I have listened to motivational speakers like Earl Nightengale and Dr. Stephen Covey, and I have attended training sessions from the best in the business like Tony Robbins and the Dale Carnegie training institute. I have learned that no matter what you do in life—career, family, service to your community—you need to be yourself. It's the essential key to your ultimate happiness.

Here's what I learned in a nutshell:

- **Be yourself.** Never try to be someone else, or change yourself just to please others. You have God-given talents that need to be shared. They are gifts that shouldn't be hidden or kept to yourself. Your gifts include your personality, your sense of humor, your ability to love, and your ability to forgive and forget.

- **Do your best in everything you do.** You owe it to yourself to give maximum effort in your work. Don't just settle for "another day at the office." Work hard each and every minute giving 110-percent effort. By delivering more that what you are getting paid to do, the victory will soon be noticed. You should never have to ask for a pay raise; it should come to you naturally when you are noticed for your extra effort.

- **As Yoda says, "There is no try. There is *do* or *not do.*"**

- **Live in "day-tight compartments."** Live and work and play for this day only, as if it may be your last. One day, it will be.

- **Count your blessings.** Appreciate the wealth you now have. Your family and your friends. The wonderful country you live in. What's this worth to you?

- **Be a nicer person.** It's more than just holding the door for someone or waving a car ahead of you at the traffic signal once in a while. It's about doing things on a regular basis to show that you really care. Return phone calls right away, talk to the other parents on the sidelines of the soccer field, and get to know the neighbor who just moved in up the street.

- **Be a better friend.** It's about being genuine and sincere. Form habits of staying in contact with your family, friends, co-workers, clients, classmates. And do more than just e-mail, text messaging, and Facebook entries. Talk to them. Understand their tone of voice and the mood they are in. That's what builds relationships. And chances are these relationships will not break.

- **Be a better spouse, soul mate, and parent to your children.** Miracles will happen in your life when you learn to show complete and utmost respect for them. Spend time doing things that they want to do, not just following your own agenda. When they see that you are totally committed to them, they will respond by showing you love and affection.

- **Share in the happiness of others.** People are happiest when they have accomplished something—however small—that they originally considered a challenge. As they expose themselves to new experiences such as establishing a new relationship, buying a new car or home, or getting a job promotion. and they seek your approval, give it to them. Say nice things and compliment them. As Dale Carnegie says: "Be genuinely interested in other people, and they will consider you to be one of their best friends."

- **Simplify your life.** Make it a point to say "no" more often. To be effective in one area of your life you may need to eliminate some of the current activities you are engaged with. You've got to give yourself time to recharge your batteries and stay fresh.

- **Share your successes with others.** It's not bragging when you have reached a pinnacle of success and are willing to bring others along with you. You've earned the right to share your experiences with your peers, co-workers, family, and friends. Remember: It's now your duty to serve and mentor others.

- **Laugh more.** Don't tread through life with a frown on your face. Learn to laugh more—at least eight times a day. Rent a funny movie, share a joke with someone, or just be plain silly for a while. LIFE IS A GAME. But don't take it all so seriously. You can make up some of your own rules, so why not squeeze a little laughter into your daily activities? Laugh at the world around you and especially laugh at yourself.

- **Teach others what you've learned.** You know a lot more about your profession than you think you know. Share stories about your experiences that you think will benefit others. You've earned the right to even brag a little about your accomplishments, as long as it's done in a way in which others can learn something. If you like to travel, show others how to travel. If you're good at investing in the stock market, show others how to invest. And if you're a good coach to your child's little league team, show others how to coach as well. That's what mentoring is all about.

- **Show someone something new.** Every day there are opportunities to share your experiences with others. If you are genuine with your approach, they will listen.

- **Don't procrastinate.** Get 'er done!

- **Clean your desk and keep your house in order.** When there's too much clutter nothing can be found. Learn to keep your entire life in order. Do not leave your workday with a cluttered mess that you'll have to deal with in the morning. Instead, finish the task at hand before you quit for the day, and file it away. Your desk should be clean of everything when you are done. Don't leave remnants lying around.

- **Know that the effort is the reward.** Remember: It's not so much about achieving the goal, reaching the quota or earning the award as it is about the amount of effort you put forth achieving it. Trophies will get dusty, but the satisfaction of knowing you worked very hard earning them will never get old. The effort is the reward. The effort is the reward!

There's truly no better way to live than when you respect yourself for what you've done and what you're now doing. The key is to create persistency in your daily life. Replace your bad habits with new and improved ones.

They don't need to be life-changing habits, just solid ones that will shape your destiny. Others will notice these things in your life and compliment you. **It will be your duty to share with them what you've learned.**

LIVING THE DREAM

The real rules of success have never changed. They've been with us for hundreds of years. You just need to know what they are for YOU, and how it makes YOU feel.

Chapter 13

BE ENGAGED

"The difference between the impossible and the possible lies in a person's determination."

TOMMY LASORDA
HALL OF FAME BASEBALL MANAGER

My Father, Charles Wallin, suffered his first heart attack at the age of 43. With five kids it really hit the family hard. Fortunately Dad survived, but his lifestyle changed forever. He wasn't able to play baseball outside with us little ones much, and I know my mother kept a close eye on him whenever he picked up a hammer or started putting shutters up on the house. Once he fell off the ladder and broke his arm. Mom and the doctors were more afraid of his heart than his injured arm.

Dad was always a pretty serious worker. He worked many years as an accountant before landing his role as registrar and assistant dean of the University of Buffalo Law School. He often held two or more jobs and did tax work on the side to pay the bills and put enough money aside for all of us to attend college. We took annual trips to Florida to visit our grandparents, but other than that he was very careful with his expenses.

Dad always dressed for success. He never wore blue jeans, and I never remember seeing him in a pair of sneakers. I remember once he took us to the beach and he wore long trousers and a white button-down shirt. That's just who he is.

What has inspired me to write about my Dad is the fact that he constantly found time to be engaged in everything he did. Certainly at his work at the law school, he spent countless hours helping young students work the struggles of their coursework and make it to graduation. What I saw was a man who cared about his job, but, more importantly, he cared about the people who needed calm and reassuring guidance.

I remember he would often get phone calls at home from law school students who didn't think they were going to pass a certain course. It was hard work. Dad would talk to them as if they were his own children and reassure them that they would make it. At his office on campus he had a couch and students knew they could come in and visit when they needed to talk face to face. I recently visited the University of Buffalo campus and found the building and the floor where he used to work. When I introduced myself to a few of the employees they were pleased to meet me. They still remember my Dad—20 years after his retirement!

COACH CHUCK

When my younger brother, Mike, was a teenager he coaxed Dad into coaching his Little League baseball team. I don't think Dad had ever coached before, but he became obsessed with teaching the boys the proper way to play the game, while striving to win at all times. It was great watching him carry his clipboard full of notes and strategies for the upcoming "big game." They were all "big games" in his mind. In his first season, he had a winning record. The second season he took the championship, defeating the bitter rival with great base-running, great pitching, and great coaching strategy.

Somewhere around this baseball time, we kids began calling Dad "Chuck." I'm not really sure why, but "Dad" just didn't fit anymore. We had seen something different about him. Perhaps it was because we were older (I was about 17 and Mike was about 13). Perhaps it was because he had taught us many great things, like how to work hard, how to save money, and how to plan for the future. Perhaps it was that we had grown up just the way he wanted, and he now expected us to be his friends, not just his children.

Whatever the reason, the name fit. And we would call him Chuck forever.

As he grew older he was forced to have open heart surgery and eventually a pacemaker and defibrillator for his weak heart. He endured a lot of pain and suffering and was forced to retire at the age of 62. Mom and Chuck were able to enjoy their retirement as they traveled the world extensively. They sat back and supported us five kids as we experienced college life and marriages and children of our own. What a life!

YOU'RE NEVER TOO OLD TO TRY SOMETHING NEW

But it doesn't end there. Even though Chuck was suffering physically he didn't stop being active. In his late 70s he decided to take piano lessons. He had always played piano in our living room and was pretty good at it. He was self-taught. But even at this stage in his life, he wanted to improve. As he took his weekly lessons he found himself getting better and better. He played for hours by himself. But again, something was missing.

At the urging of his piano teacher, he decided to volunteer at local nursing homes and hospitals. He went on a regular basis and played for the residents and patients, many whom were about his age. He played old show tunes, marching ballads and sing-alongs like "Glory, Glory Hallelujah." Sometimes the residents pulled their wheelchairs right up to him while he was playing and sang along right beside him. My mother often went along with him just for moral support, because he always wanted to perform his very best.

Recently I attended church with my parents. While we entered the facility, Mom was fixated on delivering a bag of canned goods to the local food drive—not uncommon for her. Chuck was talking to a lady who had organized a variety show at the nursing home where she worked and had enlisted him to play piano for the show. She went out of her way to thank him for his outstanding piano playing that made the show a huge success. I was in awe of my parents, and I felt so honored and blessed to be in their presence. To them it was just another day; to me it was an incredible moment.

My father has taught me a lot about being a father myself: how not to raise your voice when angry, how to carefully think before responding to an issue or concern, and how to save money and plan for the future by properly investing in the stock market and learning as much about the stock as possible before buying it.

Most important, he taught me how to always strive to do your best—at work, on the field of play, at practice sessions, and on the stage.

LIVING THE DREAM

You're never too old to try something new, and when you do, you will amaze yourself at the levels of satisfaction you receive.

PILLAR 4
In Pursuit of Caring

"Knowing others is wisdom, knowing yourself is Enlightenment."

LAU-TSU

PHILOSOPHER OF ANCIENT CHINA (6TH CENTURY BC)

Chapter 14

LEARN TO CARE

"You raise me up so I can stand on mountains. You raise me up to walk on stormy seas. I am strong when I am on your shoulder. You raise me up to more than I can be."

JOSH GROBIN
GRAMMY-NOMINATED SINGER AND SONGWRITER

THE SHARON TOWNS STORY

I met Sharon back in 1999 when I was looking to hire a telemarketer for my insurance business. I felt bad when I first saw her, she had some physical conditions that made it hard for her to walk. She explained to me that she had been employed as a legal secretary for 30 years but was forced to retire due to the rheumatoid arthritis that had developed in her hip. She was unable to stand for even a short period of time and found it impossible to sit at a desk for an extended period of time, much less eight hours a day.

I was confident in her skills and agreed to hire Sharon

and give her the flexibility of working most of her hours from home. Her job was to call our insurance clients and ask for additional sales. A few years passed, and I began to realize that Sharon had a lot more to offer than just making phone calls. I asked her if she'd like to be my bookkeeper and spend a little more time in the office. She agreed.

As I got to know Sharon better I learned that she was already a published author herself. She and her husband Dan researched and wrote a book called *Voices from the Garden* (Lantern Books, 2001), in which they told stories of vegetarian families from all over the world and how they lived. Wow! I thought to myself. This lady has a lot of talent beneath the surface. Despite her medical conditions she was doing things most people only dreamed about.

One day I asked Sharon if she would help me get started on my own book. You see, I've always had a dream to write; I just didn't know how. She began mentoring me on the work it would take to not only write, but also how to get interest from book publishers and obtain testimonials from important people. Rejection came often, but she always encouraged me to keep going and not give up. As I continued to write, Sharon assisted with research on various industry statistics. She spent time on the Internet gathering motivational quotes and statistical information that would lend credibility to the book. She listened to ideas I presented to her about a given chapter, and even though I thought they were great, she often told me to slow down and think about what I was doing.

Sharon cared. She cared about my book and the success I might have in the future as an accomplished author. But more importantly, she cared about me. She supported my dream and was going to do everything within her power to help me succeed.

CARING MOMENTS

In the early spring of 2007, Sharon suffered a stroke. Although she was still in her 50s, her body had simply given out. I remember the doctor in the hospital showing me the brain X-ray where it showed severe hemorrhage. The stroke left her paralyzed on half of her body, and she could no longer speak. The doctors didn't expect her to live. My wonderful staff—Marlene, Linda, Moe, Jonna, and Lloyd—along with Dan spent countless hours at her bedside. She could hear and understand us, but she could hardly communicate back to us. We were all very sad that this could happen to our close friend.

After a couple of weeks in the hospital Sharon showed little improvement. But suddenly I was excited to go see her. My book *In Pursuit of Business* had finally been published and I wanted Sharon to be the first person to see it. I raced through St. Joseph's Hospital hallway as fast as I could. I then entered Sharon's room and showed her the book. Without a word, we both started to cry. Tears of joy! I remember the others in the room had tears as well.

Somewhere along the way, Sharon had taught us how important it was to support each other's goals and dreams. And my dream had come true. It was one of the happiest moments of my life, even though not a word was spoken.

Sharon lived another six months, way beyond any of our expectations. She slowly regained her ability to communicate and even was able to go home for a while. But her job on this earth had been completed—not just for how she cared about me, but how she cared for everyone in her life.

LIVING THE DREAM

To love is to receive a glimpse of heaven. It's beautiful.

CHERISH LIFE

As I prepared to make a few remarks at Sharon's funeral, I went back and thought about the last Christmas we had together, before she suffered her stroke. She had been bugging the staff and me to have a very special office party where we would close the office early one day and invite our families in for some good food and drink. Although the rest of us complained that we were all pretty busy—just like every other Christmas season with shopping, traveling, and home parties—we agreed we would chip in and help Sharon with the office party. We giggled amongst ourselves as we watched her take charge of the event, not leaving any detail untouched. This obviously meant a lot to her.

When we finally locked the front office door and stopped answering the phone the party began. Sharon had asked us to arrange chairs in a circle pattern so we could all eat, drink, and talk. And we partied! Family members and close friends came in the back door and visited while the sounds of Christmas music rang throughout the building. The decorations were beautiful and the food was awesome. The look on her face was that of a proud lady. She had forced her hand and made us have this party, and it worked. She had each of us in a festive mood, surrounded by many of the important people in our lives. She beamed that day.

I wonder if Sharon really knew this would be her last Christmas. I wonder if she realized what a powerful gift she had given us. She cared about us so much. She had taught us how precious and awesome our lives really were, and that we all needed to slow down and appreciate each and every moment and each and every person in our lives.

LEARNING TO CARE

We held a small remembrance service for Sharon. We shared stories about our trip to Yankee Stadium together (she actually received a get-well card from Yankees Star Mariano Rivera and had her name highlighted on the scoreboard—she had connections!) and our early days in the insurance agency. We then played some of her favorite music, and as the Josh Groban and Chris Daughtry songs played, there wasn't a dry eye in the room. But many of us also smiled to the heavens as we knew Sharon had completed her job here on earth.

There's a country song by Kenny Chesney called "Don't

Blink" where he asks a 102 year-old man about the secret to life. *"Don't blink,"* he says. *"Trust me, friend, 100 years goes faster than you think; You better start putting first things first."*

Life passes by so fast; don't miss anything by not caring and not paying attention to the important people you love. Slow down, take it easy, and don't let the little things get you down.

Our lives really do race by—season after season and year after year. Some people enter our life and leave without much impact. Others come and make life-altering changes that will make you a stronger and more special person than you already are.

Be ready for them when you see them.

LIVING THE DREAM

"Don't cry because it's over,
smile because it happened."

DR. SEUSS (TED GEISEL)

Chapter 15

PAY IT FORWARD

"Is it possible for one idea to change the world?"

FROM THE MOVIE *PAY IT FORWARD*

THE STARFISH STORY IS ONE
THAT HAS ALWAYS BEEN CLOSE
TO MY HEART.

THE STARFISH STORY"

ORIGINAL STORY BY: LOREN EISLEY

One day a man was walking along the beach
when he noticed
a boy picking something up and gently
throwing it into the ocean.
Approaching the boy, he asked,
"What are you doing?"
The youth replied,
"Throwing starfish back into the ocean.
The surf is up and the tide is going out.
If I don't throw them back, they'll die."
"Son," the man said,"don't you realize there are miles
and miles of beach and hundreds of starfish?
You can't make a difference!"
After listening politely, the boy bent down,
picked up another starfish,
and threw it back into the surf.
Then, smiling at the man, he said—
"I made a difference for that one."

THE MOVEMENT

Every once in a while I am struck with a heartwarming story of how people help each other for no reason at all. There's the story of a plane crash in Buffalo, where tragically there were no survivors. The community banded together to show support to the victims' families, most of whom they did not know. Acts of kindness—like a home-cooked meal, attending a prayer service together, or setting up a scholarship fund—remind us of how precious life really is, and that we really do need each other.

There's a movie called *Pay it Forward,* starring Haley Joel Osment and Kevin Spacey. In the story an 11-year-old boy is challenged by his teacher to think of something BIG in his life and then take massive action to see the idea realized. The boy comes up with a simple idea of going to three people and trying to help them improve their lives—ideas like helping a homeless drug addict find a home and kick the habit, helping his teacher finding true love, and sticking up for his friend when he got bullied at the playground.

These three people would then be challenged to help three people of their own, and then they would help three people – and so on and so on. Three turns into nine, nine into twenty-seven, twenty-seven into eighty-one, and eighty-one into 243 fast. PAY IT FORWARD!

Perform three big favors for other people. It sounds pretty simple. Why can't we all do this?

WHEN SOMEONE DOES YOU A BIG FAVOR, DON'T PAY IT BACK—PAY IT FORWARD

The realm of possibility exists inside each of us. Make your friend's day by thinking of how you can help him or her—and then do it. The world will become a better place.

Traditional wisdom suggests that the person we're doing a favor for should pay us back—return the favor. It's expected, right? Our society has somehow taught us we should all expect to get paid back for our good deeds. I've been here, too. I've felt so good about helping someone that I half expect my name to be placed on the front page of the local newspaper—what a great guy, what a great deed, yippee!

Well, that's nice—but it's short-lived. More news will come and overshadow my good deed. My fifteen minutes of fame will be over.

So why not practice the pay-it-forward movement? This way the legacy continues. The feeling of satisfaction can be everlasting.

I recently met with a friend of mine from our community named James. James was struggling because the newspaper where he worked had eliminated his position. They offered him another job within the organization, but at half the pay. He was frustrated and felt trapped because he had a family to support. He talked about possibly changing careers. Being in the insurance industry myself I told him how I felt my industry was positioned in this current economy and that it may be a good opportunity for him. He began interviewing to own his own insurance agency, using me as an advisor along the way. In our subsequent conversations I assured him he could use me as a reference during his interview process, but then I'd like for him to someday find a way to help three others in some special way. Don't pay me back; pay them instead.

I'm looking forward to witnessing how James's good fortune will soon benefit others. Deep inside, I'll feel pretty good myself.

LIVING THE DREAM

"All the resources we need are in the mind."

THEODORE ROOSEVELT

ACT WITH YOUR HEART

Another example of caring is with my friend Doreen Lafleur. When Doreen was first married and beginning a family, she and her husband Jim were struggling financially to make ends meet. As a young family they decided that Doreen would quit her job and stay at home and care for their disabled child. Through that situation came the generosity of others. The special car seat, one so their son Brian could lie down in, was given to them within the first few months of the child's life, by relatives who run Harvest House in Buffalo. "It was difficult to go from being very proud and independent people to needing and accepting the generosity of others," she said. "We later paid it forward by working at a beer tent for their mission and then gave the seat back to Harvest House so it could be given to another family in need."

Later that year at Christmas she received a donation of $200 from the local Garden Club (headed up by my mother, the saint!). "We really needed this money, the front door to our house was broken and we wanted to give our 5-year old son his dream Christmas," Said Doreen. She always felt thankful for the kindness that was given to her and she promised that one day, when she was in a better position financially, she would carry the movement forward.

"Our paying the monetary gift *forward* came 15 years later, when I learned of a need and acted on what my heart wanted to do. It felt like the perfect time and opportunity. It is never too late, there will always be a person in need. The paying it forward can be in any form, not just one that mirrored the way you were helped. It is as simple as helping a family provide for their family in any way."

Doreen then became aware that many children in her own church community (as well as in other areas of the country) did not have a bed to sleep on. "I discovered that kids were sleeping on the floor because their families could not afford a bed. I thought to myself: wouldn't it be great to give them all a nice bed to sleep in?" She felt compelled to help families, similar to how she was helped in the past. She began collecting used beds and finding homes for them.

She created a program where people can donate their beds and bedding supplies. "I started slowly but it has now grown. I listened to the voice in my heart, I overcame my fears and made it happen. I knew there was a need and I had the passion and determination to pay forward what had been given to me." Her vision is countrywide and I'm confident she'll continue to help needy families for years to come.

"In every society there are 'human benchmarks'—certain individuals whose behavior becomes a role model for everyone else—shining examples that others admire and emulate. We call these individuals 'class acts.'"

DAN SULLIVAN, PRESIDENT, THE STRATEGIC COACH

HELPING OTHERS

Here are some ways you can help others:

- Help someone who is out of work find a job
- Help someone who needs a car
- Help someone who needs a babysitter
- Help someone understand their own finances better
- Help someone who is looking for love

And in return ask them to do a favor for three other people. It's possible that the work you do here may lead to amazing results.

LIVING THE DREAM

"Make happy those who are near, and those who are far will come."

CHINESE PROVERB

There's a story about a poor Scottish farmer named Fleming who saved a lad from a vicious animal attack. Had he not come along the lad would have died a slow, horrible death. The next day a fancy carriage pulled up to the farmer's humble abode. The nobleman in the carriage tried to offer the farmer money for saving his son's life, but the farmer refused. The nobleman saw the farmer's son and said, "I will provide your son with the same education as my son. No doubt he will grow to be a man of whom we will both be proud." Farmer Fleming's son graduated from St. Mary's Medical School in London and went on to become known as Sir Alexander Fleming—the discoverer of Penicillin.

But the story doesn't end there. Years later the nobleman's son was stricken with pneumonia. What saved his life? Penicillin. The name of the nobleman was LORD RANDOLPH CHURCHILL. His son was SIR WINSTON CHURCHILL.

The pay-it-forward movement can be very rewarding, whether it be in the form of charity, teaching others or inventing a product to help the next generation. Napoleon

Hill once said, *"Whatever the mind can conceive and believe, it can conceive."* Your mind is such a powerful instrument it can deliver to you amazing things. You must believe that all things are possible

You can achieve anything you want, if you have a strong enough conviction and ability to act in accordance to your faith and your God-given ability. I look forward to hearing about your success story.

LIVING THE DREAM

When you throw a pebble into the pond the ripple effect goes all the way to the shore.

Chapter 16

MAKE FRIENDS WHO WILL LAST A LIFETIME

"When the character of a person is not clear to you, look at his friends."

JAPANESE PROVERB

What's really important in life? The people we know and care about. If I asked you to name the five wealthiest people in the world, could you? Or how about the names of the last ten people who have won the Nobel prize? Or try this: Can you name the last five football Heisman trophy winners?

The point is, none of us remember the people who made headlines in the past. Sure, they are top-notch achievers. But once the dust settles, they tend to be forgotten. They are replaced by another set of high-level winners, and the world goes on and on. Accolades and certificates get old and tarnished and are quickly outdated.

The familiar-looking faces of the stars we see on television or in the movies are just that: They are faces. You don't know those people, and they don't know you. Rather, think about the important people in your own life who have made a difference in your personal development and growth. For example:

- List a few teachers who aided in your journey through school.
- Name three friends who have helped you through a difficult time.
- Think of some people who always make you feel appreciated and special.
- Name five people you enjoy spending time with.
- Name some people you know who you would consider a hero.

LIVING THE DREAM

You already know the most important people in your life.

THE JOURNEY AND THE DESTINATION

When I graduated from Binghamton University back in the mid-1980s I was in no mood to begin working a real job. I wanted to see the world, you know—explore and sow my wild oats. My college roommate, Mike Piccirillo, and I set out on a cross-country journey from New York to California. We traveled any way we could: by car, by bus, by subway, and by foot. (Yes, I admit to hitchhiking. Although I wouldn't recommend it today, especially when talking to my teenagers, at that time it was a cheap and effective way to get from one place to the next.)

I kept a journal with me so I could log our activities and capture my thoughts and feelings along the way.

Mike and I took our time as we made stops in Chicago, Des Moines, Denver, and Salt Lake City. We kept our expenses low by using backpacks and tents rather than motels. We ate cheap, things like macaroni and cheese (cooked over an open campfire), tuna fish, and bread. We became vegetarians simply because we couldn't afford to buy meat. We saved our money for important things like bus fare and beer. We spent a few days in Reno, Nevada, but were afraid the casinos would take more money than give.

We arrived in California via Lake Tahoe and simply took in the beauty of the land. We camped at a site right on the lake, with a view of the snow-capped mountains off in the distance. Mike and I spent a few days talking with other campers; some would ask us to have dinner with them at their campsite. They might have felt sorry for us when they heard about the type of food we had been eating.

Our next stop was San Francisco, and then down the coast with no real timetable of where we wanted to be. We slept on the California beaches for one dollar a night. Couldn't beat that! I vividly remember following along with a whole bunch of Grateful Dead groupies, who were following the band everywhere they went. It was cool meeting these people and learning their stories. Many were hard-working citizens who had taken the summer off in order to sleep on the beach and party with their friends. They obviously had set their priorities in order of what they wanted to experience in life.

We continued our journey hiking through the artichoke fields of Castroville and made small talk with the local town folks who shared with us the history of their land and how the migrant workers had come for the picking season. We took local bus rides as far as they would go, sometimes staying on the bus long after the last passenger had exited, just so we could chat with the bus driver about the local lore.

THE PIZZA DUDE

I remember one night Mike and I were settling in at our Pismo Beach campsite as the sun began to set. We were looking forward to a quiet and restful night under the beautiful ocean sky. Then, all of a sudden, a guy rolled into the site next to us, riding on a bike. He was all alone. He created enough noise and uproar that the entire campground must have awakened. He turned up his little music machine very loud and invited anyone within his reach to come out and join him. He was having pizza delivered—

and he wanted to share it.

Mike and I immediately were no longer tired. We jumped up, grabbed a few cold beers, and jogged over to meet our new friend. We built a fire so we could see each other better and get to know each other. We found out his name was Tom and he was riding his bike down the California coast, going nowhere in particular. His real mission was to meet as many people along the way, tell jokes and stories, and share his dreams. It worked. Tom made an impression on me that I will never forget. As a young man himself, he had found his passion.

Sure enough, about an hour later, we saw the "Fat Albert's Pizza" truck circling the grounds looking for a guy named Tom.

The next morning as I emerged from my tent I looked over to the area where we had spent the previous evening laughing and joking. Our friend had already left.

THE BUS DRIVER

During the same trip Mike and I boarded a local bus near Salinas, California. We were immediately greeted by Cal, the big bus driver with an even bigger smile. He saw us carrying our backpacks and knew we were not from that area of the country. We really weren't sure where we were going; we just wanted to go south, closer to Los Angeles, where perhaps where we would settle down and look for work.

He charged us the $1.50 fare and told us to sit in the front of the bus, so he could talk to us along the way. He immediately engaged us in a conversation about our background, our education, and where we were going. He then shared with us the history of the area, and pointed out various spotlights of the area, mainly agriculture and how that state uses a lot of migrant workers in the fields to pick the crops. I posted this entry in my journal:

"Cal may not have the best job or the best of all backgrounds, but he is truly a happy man. He is happy with his job, his home, his life and HIS California. An educated man, he claims he is wealthier as a bus driver than by holding another type of career job. I don't know if this is true nor do I really care, I just think this guy wants to be around people. And when he is around people—perhaps he IS a very wealthy man, in many ways."

When we reached the end of his route Mike and I were the only ones left on the bus. As we said goodbye to Cal, he shook our hands with more care and delight than I've ever seen before in my life. Although I'll never see him again in my life, I know he was a true friend at a time when we really needed it.

As I tell these stories about my country-wide journey I must tell you that it can never be relived or repeated. The places still exist, but the memory I have created is mine. It can never be taken away or changed. Only Mike or I have the ability to tell the story the way it happened, because we were there, and we met these people along the way.

But the trip changed my life.

It's the people in your life who make up who you are. It's not about going to lavish and expensive places, rather it's about enjoying the experience in your own way. Go out and meet people—young, old, local, or traveler—it doesn't matter. I try to teach this to my teenage children almost every day I'm with them. Form relationships, make them meaningful, and build bonds that will last a lifetime.

LIVING THE DREAM

Be sure to take time to care about others you meet. Get to know others in an intimate way. Learn something about them that you never knew before. You will build relationships that will last a lifetime.

As a shy person growing up I limited myself to only socializing with people I knew well, like family and classmates. That was my comfort zone, and I liked it. As I grew older and started opening my eyes to other people I saw what they had to offer. I realized I was missing this critical area of my life.

To this day I relish the opportunity to meet new people. I use my experience to get a conversation flowing with strangers quite simply and with ease. I have learned to ask questions and show genuine interest in the other person, and then I sit back and listen.

MEET THREE NEW PEOPLE EACH DAY

"It's never crowded along the extra mile."

DR. WAYNE DYER
AUTHOR OF *HOW TO GET WHAT YOU REALLY, REALLY, REALLY, REALLY WANT*

You can never have too many friends. And you have opportunities to meet people all day long:

- Say hello to the person next to you in line at the grocery store.
- Join a church club, country club, or other community group that you are interested in.
- Take a different route when you drive to work or school or shopping. Stop by areas you've never been before and see who's there.
- Volunteer to coach youth sports—whether your kid plays or not.
- Begin a conversation with someone you've seen at the gym but never spoken to.
- Wear a shirt with a logo from your favorite sports team. It may prompt a conversation with a fan or a foe (in good nature I hope!).
- Ask a co-worker that you don't know very well to join you for lunch.

LIVING THE DREAM

"Set a goal to meet three new people a day—which adds up to over 1,000 in a year. There's an abundance of people out there looking to be your friend. You just have to open the door for them."

MARK TWAIN

(1835-1910) AMERICAN AUTHOR AND HUMORIST

Chapter 17

BEST FRIENDS

"To get the full value of joy you must have somebody to divide it with."

MARK TWAIN

(1835-1910) AMERICAN AUTHOR AND HUMORIST

THE CHURCH, THE RECEPTION, AND THE HONEYMOON

The story I'm about to tell is the truth. I swear it is; you can't make up something like this.

Marilyn and I met in the in early 1985. I was working for Coca-Cola at the time, earning minimum wage stocking shelves at local supermarkets. She was the bulk food manager at Tops Supermarket in Niagara Falls, New York. I had just returned from my cross-country adventure and wanted to put my college education to work. I was quite focused on my new job even though it was only an entry-level position.

I must admit I wasn't observant to the things going on around me as I performed my work. My goal was to visit a half dozen or so supermarkets each day and prepare the soft drink shelves and displays to sell my product. I would cart enough 2-liter bottles, 16-ounce glasses, and 12-ounce cans from the Coke truck to keep the store in stock until my next visit a few days later. This was also the time period when America had begun collecting empty bottles and recycling them. Many stores were not very equipped to handle this new duty, so I had my work cut out for me.

I never really noticed that Marilyn and her girlfriends were checking me out.

I must admit I did hear announcements and laughter coming over the loud speaker at my Niagara Falls store location, but I had no idea it was aimed at me. Then one day, Tony the manager came up to me while I was in the beverage aisle finishing up some paperwork. The words he said to me I will remember forever:

"Peter, have you been paying attention to the lady who's been talking to you over the loud speaker? Her name is Marilyn and she's single. She's a very pretty girl and she thinks you are cute. Why don't you ask her out on a date? Oh, and one more thing. If you two ever get married be sure to invite me to the wedding."

I stood in silence for a few moments and then I saw her. She was standing at the end of the aisle with her two girlfriends. She gave me a little wave and that was it. The romance had begun.

We dated for a year and a half before setting a wedding date in the fall of 1986. We invited 150 of our family, best friends, and co-workers, and of course we invited Tony the manager.

THE CHURCH

St. Christopher's on Niagara Falls Boulevard. It was an emotional scene, as my dad had just recovered from his open-heart surgery. We were so happy to have him there. My college roommates and childhood buddies were all there. I was the first one among these groups to get married. I wore a stylish Royal Blue tuxedo with white pants and white shoes (this was the Miami Vice era, remember?). Marilyn walked down the aisle in a gorgeous gown befit for a queen. It was a scene I'll never forget.

THE RECEPTION

The Cavalier was a very nice restaurant just a few miles up the road. Since our wedding was on a Friday night we were all in the mood to party. The food was delicious, the music was awesome, and the open bar was flowing with patrons. As the night wore on my brother Mike (the best man) and Marilyn's sister Martha (the maid of honor) broke out the dark sunglasses and began dancing on top of the tables. Soon, we all joined in and the event became legendary.

THE HONEYMOON

The Jack Tar Village Resort in the Grand Bahamas. The day after the reception we flew to the Caribbean to this private resort. For one week we relaxed on the ocean with its clean white sand and deep blue water. The highlight (I should say the lowlight) of our trip occurred when I casually leaned against an outside stainless steel refrigerator while wearing my dripping wet bathing suit. I was immediately "shocked"! The wiring obviously was not grounded properly. Luckily, Marilyn grabbed my limp arm and pulled me away from the electric jolt. She saved my life!

The interesting conclusion to this story is that a short time after our wedding all three facilities that we spent so much time preparing for were gone.

- The church burned down as the result of an arson fire—a mystery that was never solved.
- The restaurant also had a fire in the kitchen that destroyed the entire facility.
- The resort in the Bahamas was closed down due to maintenance and health code violations (obviously!). The entire facility was later demolished.

Our church, our reception and our honeymoon were gone. Or were they?

LIVING THE DREAM

"Most folks are about as happy as they make up their minds to be."

ABRAHAM LINCOLN

MEMORIES

What remains are the memories we created: our relationship with Tony the manager who originally introduced us to each other. Our loved ones, including aunts, uncles, and friends who have since passed away. Our memory of dancing on the tables in a wild celebration of love and joy. And certainly the gift of life Marilyn gave me by saving me from electrocution.

That's what's important. That's what we remember, and that's what we'll always cherish.

THERE'S MORE TO LIFE

God has a plan for all of us. We just need to have faith in Him and trust where we are going.

Life is about more than bricks and mortar. It's about more than food and drink. It's about more than fancy tuxedos and one-of-a-kind gowns. It's about more than travel and luxury resorts. It's about faith, love, and connection.

Marilyn and I often laugh about the fact that today all of the components of our wedding are now gone. We can't go back to physically visit these places. They no longer exist. What we can do is hold each other and remember the day and that we shared it with the most important 150 people in our lives at the time. This is what we now share with our children. And this is what our foundation of marriage is all about. We know we can't always control what happens in the world around us. But we can control our response: the way we live, the way we pray, the way we dream, and the way we love.

TAKE A LEAP!

"Come to the edge, He said.
They said: We are afraid.
Come to the edge, He said.
They came, He pushed them,
And they flew..."

GUILLAME APOLLINAIRE
AVANT-GARDE FRENCH POET

LIVING THE DREAM

Take a Leap! Have faith in God and everything around you. It will no longer seem difficult.

Chapter 18

BE GRATEFUL

"Showing appreciation can make someone's day, even change a life. Your willingness to put it into word is all that is necessary."

PETER WALLIN

Several years ago I heard the following poem, and it had such an impact on me that I immediately said a prayer of thanks for everything that has been given to me and my family. I know deep in my heart that I have been blessed with good health, good fortunes, and the ability to love and be loved. I am thankful that I now fully understand and appreciate that nothing in my life is guaranteed. I must appreciate everything as I see it here and now.

"OH GOD, FORGIVE ME WHEN I WHINE"

Today upon a bus, I saw a lovely girl with golden hair, I envied her…she seemed so joyful…and I wished I was as happy. When suddenly she rose to leave, I saw her hobble down the aisle; she had one leg and wore a crutch; but as she passed…a smile!

Oh, God, forgive me when I whine, I have two legs. The world is mine!

I stopped to buy some candy. The lad who sold it had such charm. I talked with him. He seemed so glad. If I were late 't would do no harm. And as I left he said to me, "I thank you. You have been so kind. It's nice to talk with folks like you. You see," he said, "I'm blind."

Oh, God, forgive me when I whine, I have two eyes. The world is mine.

Later, while walking down the street, I saw a child with eyes of blue. He stood and watched the others play. He did not know what to do. I stopped for a moment, and then I said, "Why don't you join the others, dear?" He looked ahead without a word, and then I knew he could not hear.

Oh, God, forgive me when I whine. I have two ears. The world is mine.

With feet to take me where I want to go, with eyes to see the sunset's glow, with ears to hear what I should know…

Oh, God, forgive me when I whine. I'm blessed indeed. The world is mine.

—AUTHOR UNKNOWN

I've shared a lot of personal and emotional stories throughout this book. I've told you all of it in order to tell you this: *be grateful for everything you now have in your life!* Appreciate where you have come from and the possibilities of where you are going.

LIVING THE DREAM

Being grateful allows us to be happy. Being happy allows us to fulfill our dreams—to accomplish what we set out to do in our lives.

The dream you are now living is your own creation—not mine. I have simply shared personal stories from my own life to get you to think about what you can do with your life. You now have the ability and the power to create your own riches and your own happiness. Remember that your ultimate happiness is more internal than it is external: It's how you feel about your life each and every day.

IMAGINE

Using your imagination, think about the areas of your life that are most important to you. See yourself living a life of full of delight, where dreams can and do come true:

- Imagine that you are able to express yourself openly and honestly to everyone you know. You aren't afraid to hug someone and to say "I love you."

- Imagine yourself being grateful for everything you have been given. Some of the things you prayed for may not have been given to you. Like Garth Brooks sings: "Some of God's greatest gifts are unanswered prayers." We can't have everything we ask for in this life. But we can appreciate the things we have, the health that we have, the home and good fortune we've earned, and the people who have come into our lives.

- Imagine not worrying about being judged by others. It's important to hear what others are saying, but don't be offended by it. You can't control what they are saying, but you can control how you respond. Your response will define who you really are.

- Imagine you have the ability to see things as they are and you appreciate what it took to get here. It's not important to focus on what's wrong, rather, focus on what's right. You should be proud of your education, your career, your home, and your family. Say a prayer of thanks each day for what God has given you—and appreciate it all!

- Imagine living your life without fear of expressing your dreams. You know what you want and who you want to share it with. You are free to change your life any way you want to. You can say "yes" when you want, and you can say "no" when you want.

- Imagine living your life where you are able to forgive others and let go of any judgment you have. You no longer have to prove yourself right or prove others wrong. Just be happy, and let it go.
- Imagine you enjoy your career so much you look forward to Mondays as much as you look forward to Fridays.
- Imagine living your life without fear of taking a risk. Be willing to try something new, meet someone new, and not be worried about rejection.
- Imagine you love yourself just the way you are. You feel good about your body, your intellectual mind, your personality and your beliefs. You walk with a posture of confidence because you are real—and you love the real you.
- Imagine you understand what true love really means and that you care for another person's happiness more than your own.
- Imagine what your own book would look like. Concentrate on the positives—the Cloud 9 stuff!—and not the negatives.

KNOWING THE FOUR PILLARS

Don Miguel Ruiz, author of *The Four Agreements* (Amber-Allen Publishing, 1997), says: "Only love has the ability to put you in a state of bliss. When you experience bliss you will know that heaven on earth is truth—that heaven truly exists." Once you know that heaven exists and once you know that it is possible to stay there, it's up to you to make the effort to get there.

Yes, it is possible to live your life in a state of mastery. It can be learned, just like you learned math and science and history in school. It will take effort and commitment, but it can be done. Trust me.

You owe it to yourself…and you deserve the chance to feel what a successful life is all about. By creating a proper balance in your life you will have mastered the four pillars of Living, Giving, Sharing, and Caring in your own way, and on your own terms.

Feel it…live it…master it…savor it! God Bless.